C0-BVO-270

VOID

Library of
Davidson College

THE CONTOURS
OF CHURCH AND STATE
IN THE THOUGHT OF
JOHN PAUL II

By George Huntston Williams

Institute of Church-State Studies - Baylor University
Monograph Series

BAYLOR UNIVERSITY PRESS ● Waco, Texas 76798

Copyright © 1983 by

Institute of Church-State Studies

Baylor University, CSB 380, Waco, Texas 76798

261.7
W723c

85-9061

All rights reserved

Printed in the United States of America

Library of Congress Catalog Card Number 83-171724

International Standard Book Number 0-918954-41-X

Contents

Preface

This volume is a careful and comprehensive examination of the thought and actions of Pope John Paul II concerning church-state relations. A distinguished church historian and author of a wide range of significant studies in church history, George Huntston Williams brings to this volume years of personal acquaintance with the subject of this study and with the history of the church in Poland. The author was one of the few persons who predicted the elevation of Karol Cardinal Wojtyla of Cracow to pontiff and chief pastor of the Roman Catholic Church. The author's *The Mind of John Paul II: Origins of His Thought and Action* (New York: Seabury Press, 1981) has been widely praised for its erudition and insightful analyses.

Born in Wadowice, Poland, on 18 May 1920, Wojtyla, following his ordination in 1946, received a doctorate in divinity and held the chair of ethics at the Catholic University of Lublin. Named bishop in 1958, archbishop of Cracow in 1963, and cardinal by Pope Paul VI in 1967, Wojtyla became pope on 16 October 1978. From its beginning, his pontificate has assumed a special significance for Catholics and non-Catholics alike. The first non-Italian pope in 455 years, the first pontiff from a communist nation, and already the most widely traveled pope in all of history, John Paul II's thought on church and state and his relations with various nation-states and current political movements amply warrant the special attention given this study by the author.

The two principal essays of this volume were originally published in *Journal of* CHURCH *and* STATE. In addition to these essays, a "Bibliographical Essay" has been especially prepared for this volume. This monograph is published in order to serve an even wider readership and to make available the subject of this study in one volume.

June 1983   James E. Wood, Jr.

ERRATUM

Page 5, fn 15: Because of its length, the article mentioned did not appear in *Mid-Stream* but in *Harvard Theological Review* 76 (January 1983):1ff.

John Paul II's Concepts of Church, State, and Society[1]

GEORGE HUNTSTON WILLIAMS

On 16 October 1982 the Polish pontiff John Paul II celebrated the close of his first four years as pope. A second phase of his pontificate had not opened at the time of the attempt upon his life on 13 May 1981. While a protracted recovery obliged him to give up for a season his strenuous schedule, by the end of his convalescence he had promulgated *Laborem exercens* of 14 September 1981, which followed in less than a year his second encyclical, *Dives in misericordia* of 30 November 1980. This third, on labor, he had drafted in Polish while recuperating in the Gemelli Polyclinic. He was so moved by the world's outpouring of admiration and affection that he had come to understand the assault as a cosuffering with Jesus Christ, and he willingly offered the encyclical "for the healing of the Church and the world."[2]

On 13 December 1981 he faced the imposition of martial law in his homeland and dashed hopes for the social, economic, and ecclesiastical achievements of Lech Walesa, whom he had counseled. After conferring with Archbishop Józef Glemp, primate of Poland, and Archbishops Franciszek Cardinal Macharski of Cracow and

GEORGE HUNTSTON WILLIAMS (A.B., St. Lawrence University; B.D., Meadville Theological School, University of Chicago Divinity School; Th.D., Union Theological Seminary) is Hollis Professor of Divinity Emeritus, Harvard University, Cambridge, Massachusetts. Author and editor of many books including *The Radical Reformation* (1962), *Thomas Hooker: Writings in England and Holland, 1626-1633* (1975), *The Polish Brethren, 1601-1685* (2 vols., 1980), and *The Mind of John Paul II: Origins of His Thought and Action* (1981), his articles have appeared in *Archive for Reformation History*, *Church History*, *Harvard College Library Bulletin*, *Harvard Theological Review*, *Journal of Church and State*, *Mennonite Quarterly Review*, and others.

1. A companion essay on John Paul II's thoughts and actions concerning church-state relations, "John Paul II's Relations with Non-Catholic States and Current Political Movements," appears in the Winter 1983 issue of *JCS*. Under a slightly different title the substance of these two essays was given as a single paper at the spring meeting of the American Society of Church History and as a J. M. Dawson Lecture on Church and State at Baylor University, 3 April 1981. The original has been revised, expanded, and updated to bring the account through autumn 1982.

2. Concerning the attempted assassination of the pope, see *L'Osservatore Romano*, 18-19 May 1981, p. 1. For the author's reaction to the attempted assassination, see George Huntston Williams, "Why John Paul II Is Vulnerable," *New York Times*, Late ed., 14 May 1981, p. A27. The author is persuaded that the pope sent an admonitory letter to Leonid Brezhnev on 23 February 1981 about Solidarity and that the KGB had nothing to do with the attempt on the pope's life on 13 May 1981. It is known that the papal legation for a nuclear freeze was especially well received by Brezhnev on 14 December 1981.

Henryk Gulbinowicz of Wroclaw, John Paul set out for a six-day pilgrimage to four countries in Africa from 12 to 19 February 1982, his second trip to Africa. On 28 February 1982 he called for an end to all foreign influence through arms and advisors in El Salvador and endorsed the policy of the Salvadoran bishops. He was in Portugal from 12 to 15 May 1982 and was moved to pay his respects to Mary of Fatima, the appearance of whom to shepherd children on 13 May 1917 and the annual feast thereof he related to his miraculous escape from death in St. Peter's Square.

After much hesitation, John Paul found by 26 May 1982 a formula by which he could carry out his long promised visit to the United Kingdom by not seeing the prime minister and by seeing the queen only in her capacity as supreme governor of the Anglican Church, promising the Argentineans a compensatory visit. Accordingly, he was in England, Scotland, and Wales for a pastoral and ecumenical pilgrimage from 28 May to 2 June 1982 and in Buenos Aires on 11 and 12 June 1982. He addressed in Geneva the International Labor Organization on 15 June 1982; this was the first time on a journey abroad he did not kiss the tarmac at the airport, explaining that he came solely as a head of state. He reluctantly put off his visit to Czestochowa for 26 August 1982, the sixth centenary of the translation of the Icon of the Black Madonna, invoked since 1658 as queen of Poland. He received Yasser Arafat on 15 September 1982. On 8 October his socioeconomic and political strategy for Poland was utterly overturned when parliament outlawed Solidarity. He received Maronite (Catholic) President Amin Gemayel of Lebanon on 21 October, after Gemayel had made clear in the U.N. and in Washington his intentions to insist that Israeli forces leave his lacerated land before all others. On 31 October the pope set out for Spain to honor Saint Teresa of Avila on the fourth centenary of her death, a pilgrimage postponed from nearer the festal date of 15 October because John Paul had created a parliamentary crisis concerning abortion, one that called forth new parliamentary elections.

In all the discourses and writings of John Paul II, prepapal and papal, something new and distinctive is happening to the categories and terms so basic to understanding church-state relations.[3] Vatican II itself, of course, went far toward redefining the Catholic Church and society in two great constitutions, *Lumen gentium* and *Gaudium et spes*. Karol Wojtyla was the only council father to have written, as cardinal, a major systematic work on the Council, *Sources of Re-*

---

3. See George Huntston Williams, *The Mind of John Paul: Origins of His Thought and Action* (New York: Seabury Press, 1981), pp. 126-39, 210-18; see also below, fn. 18.

newal.[4] Therein he stressed these two of the sixteen documents of the Council. He was, in fact, a major reviser of portions of *Gaudium et spes.*[5] Now, as pope, he quarries in the compressed strata of this great mountain of conciliar experience and thought, as earlier canonists did in working with the *Corpus Iuris Canonici*[6] and as he himself will soon do with the New Code of Canon Law.[7] The Polish pontiff thinks conceptually and systematically. One can distinguish, in his cascade of communications, at least nine meanings for church, three or four of which he relates actually or ideally to the state, which also has various definitions.[8]

THE NINE MEANINGS OF CHURCH IN JOHN PAUL II

Most commonly, John Paul means by church that body of which he is juridically and spiritually the head, the Roman Catholic Church with its (Uniate) Catholic Oriental jurisdictions. The New Code of Canon Law, reflecting some of the achievements of Vatican II, gives prominence to the term *communio* as both communion and intimate community but retains much of the hierarchical imagery of the church as *corpus Christi mysticum* and depends, much less than one might expect, on that of the church as the *populus Dei*, the royal priestly people pilgrimaging in time, an image so prominent at Vatican II.[9]

---

4. Karol Wojtyla, *Sources of Renewal: The Implementation of the Second Vatican Council*, trans. P. S. Falla (San Francisco: Harper and Row, 1980), translation of the Polish original, *U podstaw odnowy: Studium o realizacji Vaticanum II* (Cracow: Polskie Towarzystwo Teologiczne, 1972).

5. Williams, *The Mind of John Paul II*, pp. 179-82. For the final, full text of *Gaudium et spes*, see Walter M. Abbott, S.J., ed., *The Documents of Vatican II* (New York: Herder and Herder, Association Press, 1966), pp. 199-308; for *Lumen gentium*, see Abbott, *The Documents of Vatican II*, pp. 14-101.

6. For a short history of canon law, with specific reference to the *Corpus Iuris Canonici* of 1917, see *New Catholic Encyclopedia*, s.v. "Canon Law, History of."

7. Jurists and lawyers have been revising the *Corpus Iuris Canonici* since John XXIII's pontificate (see *Acta Apostolicae Sedis* 51 [Fall 1959]:68). Much literature has appeared concerning the New Code of Canon Law, upon which John Paul will concentrate beginning Advent 1982; more recent literature of interest includes "La révision du Code de droit canon: Communiqué de la présidence de la Commission pontificale," *La Documentation Catholique* 78 (6 December 1981):1067-69; Pericle Cardinal Felici, "In Pontificia Universitate Gregoriana, die 7 novembris 1981 Cardinalis Pericles Felici, XI Cursum renovationis canonicae pro Iudicibus inaugurando, haec verba fecit," *Communicationes* 13 (December 1981):447-49; and Felipe Gómez, S.J., "The New Canon Law Is Coming," *East Asian Pastoral Review* 19 (1982):84-90.

8. John Paul defines *ecclesia* within an intensified eschatological context, in a mood akin in some utterances to medieval conventual and heretical and to modern sectarian warnings and prognostications about the wiles of Antichrist and the Second Advent of Christ. For comments on this related subject, see George Huntston Williams, "The Ecumenical Intentions of John Paul II," *Harvard Theological Review* 75 (April 1982):141-77.

9. For Karol Wojtyla's appropriation of the term *populus Dei* (the People of God) at Vatican

A second important meaning of church, as a consequence of Vatican II, is as local parish. Few non-Catholics are aware of the extent to which a veritable "congregationalism" has taken hold in Catholicism, with the election of parish councils in the industrialized world not infrequently headed by women, and with full lay participation in the liturgy and often more readings from the scriptural lectionary and more hymns than in many Protestant services. Although the territorial parish has not disappeared, Catholics have much more choice than before concerning the local church they attend.[10] It is, moreover, out of this church from below, the church of the people, that the radical religio-social "base community"—Catholic, socialist, communitarian—emerged, the ecclesial *novum* of liberation theology.

Third, there are national or regional churches under their episcopal conferences. It is extraordinary that Vatican II could finally accomplish what the Reformation had already achieved, the vernacularization of worship and the full recovery of Scripture, without schismatic nationalization, although small threats to papal obedience still remain, from the still autonomous majority Catholic Church in China to the Tridentine integralists, like the followers of disciplined Archbishop Marcel Lefebvre, who rejects Vatican II.[11] It was a disgruntled rogue priest of this schism (a priest since repudiated, of course, by Lefebvre) who tried to bayonet the pope at Fatima on 13 May 1982.

The fourth meaning of church in Vatican II and for John Paul II is as the community of the baptized. The pope makes this point always in his usually brief speeches to non-Catholic Christians, stressing the Eucharist, however, as the sacrament of complete unity.[12]

A fifth meaning, more evident in the theologically courageous documents of Vatican II than in the communications of John Paul himself, is as the elect people of Israel before the first advent of Christ. Augustin Cardinal Bea was responsible, in part, for embedding this idea in the appropriate documents, doughty German Jesuit

---

II, see Williams, *The Mind of John Paul II*, p. 169, fn. 14, which quotes Wojtyla's first intervention as printed in *Acta Synodalia Sacrosancti Concilii Oecumenici Vaticani II*, 4 vols. in 20 pts., vol. 2, pt. 3 (Vatican City: Typis Polyglottis Vaticanis, 1970-77), p. 155.

10.   On the subject of Catholic "congregationalism," see David N. Power, O.M.I., *Gifts That Differ: Lay Ministries Established and Unestablished*, Studies in the Reformed Rites of the Catholic Church, vol. 8 (New York: Pueblo Publishing Co., 1980).

11.   Concerning the relation between the pope and Archbishop Lefebvre, see Williams, *The Mind of John Paul II*, pp. 302-3.

12.   Williams, *The Mind of John Paul II*, pp. 329-41; Williams, "The Ecumenical Intentions of John Paul II"; George Huntston Williams, "The Ecumenism of John Paul II," *Journal of Ecumenical Studies* 19 (Fall 1982).

professor of Old Testament that he was. The idea would not have been embraced by the Council, however, but for the pervasive influence of Protestantism, particularly of its reformulation in the writings of Karl Barth. Whereas the Catholic Church still, liturgically, marks the birth of the church at Pentecost, classical Protestants of the sixteenth century thought of the church of the elect as invisibly continuous with the people of the Old Covenant, conceiving, in contrast to Catholics and Radical Reformers, of but one covenant in two dispensations.[13] Barth's rethinking of these doctrines, in stressing the election and predestination of the community of faith—Israel and the church—more than that of the sainted individual, helped the fathers of Vatican II to see both continuity with Israel and Israel's ongoing role in the present, views most notably apparent in their utterances on the relation of Christianity to Judaism.[14]

Sixth, and more inclusive, is the church as the church of Abel, in effect, as humanity. The Polish pope stresses this emphasis of Vatican II without using the phrase. Indeed, he quotes over and over again the passages in the conciliar documents, which in turn rest on Irenaeus[15] and other church fathers, that state humankind was potentially saved in Christ, every person, whether he knows it or not. The conciliar documents and the pope's three encyclicals and other related utterances on redemption, mercy, and work nevertheless remain somewhat ambiguous as to whether the decisive saving act was wrought in the Incarnation of the eternally begotten Son of God as Jesus Christ, the Lord of the church and of the worlds, or whether salvation was wrested from the Father by expiation in the Crucifixion and the Resurrection of the Son, or whether the "Satisfaction of the love of the Father"[16] by Christ was merely the confirmation, as it were, of the original intention of the Triune God to save all of mankind, i.e., whether divine mercy preceded the Fall. No single theory of the Atonement has ever been made into Catholic dogma, and even in his first encyclical, *Redemptor hominis,* John Paul construed potential salvation of all human beings as grounded in one of these moments, sometimes stressing one moment, some-

---

13. The first classical Protestant to do this systematically was Heinrich Bullinger (1504-75) of Zurich.
14. Williams, *The Mind of John Paul II,* pp. 100, 173, 277.
15. Ibid., pp. 99, 168, 179-80, 187, 245, 274. There is a related christological thrust within the World Council of Churches; see George Huntston Williams, "The Assembly at Vancouver in Historical Perspective," *Mid-Stream: An Ecumenical Journal* 21 (January 1983).
16. This phrase is taken from John Paul's 1979 inaugural encyclical *Redemptor hominis* and is available in English as *The Redeemer of Man* (Boston: Daughters of St. Paul, 1979). For a discussion of the encyclical, see Williams, *The Mind of John Paul II,* pp. 305-11.

times the others (depending in part on the liturgical season), sometimes all moments as inextricably bound together in the divine plan.[17] Connected with this church of Abel or all humanity is the pope's own quite distinctive enlargement of the concept of the global neighbor, which he first worked out in *The Acting Person*,[18] and possibly, his feeling that the church of Mary is more capacious and less rigorous in its initial requirements than the hierarchical church of her Son, that she is the mother of humanity and peace.[19]

The seventh meaning of church is quite unexpected. In the decree on the training of priests, *Optatam totius* (§2), Vatican II spoke of the family as "a first seminary."[20] John Paul has carried the idea much further and speaks increasingly of the *ecclesiola*, "the domestic church," "the church of the home." His third book was *Love and Responsibility*,[21] wherein he pictured the family as preparing the offspring of parental love for the place where the road of

17. Williams, *The Mind of John Paul II*, pp. 305-11.
18. Karol Wojtyla, *The Acting Person*, ed. Anna-Teresa Tymieniecka, trans. Andrzej Potocki, Analecta Husserliana, vol. 10 (Dordrecht, The Netherlands: D. Reidel Publishing Co., 1979), the "definitive" translation of the Polish original, *Osoba i Czyn* (Cracow: Polskie Towarzystwo Teologiczne, 1969). Chapter seven of this work contains an important clarification of Karol Wojtyla's social thought in relation to his view of the person, not only to the idea of the global neighbor. The best assessment of the whole book, but without much attention to this last chapter, is Josef Seifert, "Karol Cardinal Wojtyla (Pope John Paul II) as Philosopher and the Cracow/Lublin School of Philosophy," *Aletheia* 2 (1981):130-99.

   The Acting Person, upon which Tymieniecka had "collaborated" with the author, appeared in a still more authoritative German version entitled *Person und Tat* (Freiburg: Herder, 1982), a literal rendering of the 1969 Polish title; this version is purportedly abreast of the author's own "second" updated (but unpublished) Polish edition and contains a concluding word by Andrzej Poltawski. As there are other prepapal writings of Wojtyla's on society and the state, with more than one version circulating in English, it is well to state their relationships. In *The Acting Person* itself there are two versions of chapter seven, the original translation by Potocki, which appears as an appendix, and the same chapter revised by Tymieniecka in collaboration with the author, who, however, on becoming pope did not have time to check the agreed-upon revisions in English—hence the editor's inclusion of both versions in the same volume. Evidently dissatisfied with Tymieniecka's work, Alfred Bloch and George T. Czuczka translated and edited portions of the Polish original in *Toward a Philosophy of Praxis* (New York: Crossroad, 1981). Pages 30-56 of this edition equal, with many ellipses, the substance of the last chapter of *Osoba i Czyn*, which Bloch and Czuczka translate as *The Self and the Act*, thus avoiding Tymieniecka and Potocki's translated title. There are, therefore, three English versions of that portion of Wojtyla's book most directly concerned with society. There are, moreover, two English versions of Wojtyla's "Osoba: podmiot i wspólnota," *Roczniki Filozoficzne-Etyka* 24 (1976):5-39; the essay has appeared as *The Controversy About Man*, in *Toward a Philosophy of Praxis*, pp. 12-23, and as "The Person: Subject and Community," *The Review of Metaphysics* 33 (December 1979):273-308. For some comments on Wojtyla's chapter seven, see Williams, *The Mind of John Paul II*, pp. 210-18; for a related work by Wojtyla, see fn. 34 below. For the pope's thought in general but with society and church-state relations included in the essays, see Ronald Lawler, O.F.M., and James V. Schall, S.J., eds., *The John Paul Synthesis*, 3 vols. (Chicago: Franciscan Herald Press, 1982).

19. Williams, *The Mind of John Paul II*, pp. 246-47, 279-84.
20. For the text of *Optatam totius*, see Abbott, *The Documents of Vatican II*, pp. 437-57.
21. Karol Wojtyla, *Love and Responsibility*, trans. H. T. Willetts (New York: Farrar, Straus

pilgrimage eventually forks for Christians: one larger road for most, that into marriage; the other, smaller, the road into the priesthood and the convent.[22] This "domestic church" and its political role the pope explained more explicitly in his apostolic exhortation of 22 November 1981, *Familiaris consortio.*[23] The "domestic church" constitutes the *ordo coniugatorum,* in which is fostered "a vertical transcendence" of the sovereign person over self and purely emotive nature in relation to the most intimately involved other person in one's life of faithful conjugal unity.

An eighth conception of church in John Paul, never expressly so called, is as the "ecclesial communion" of personal bonds that binds all Catholic bishops with the pope in collegiality.[24] John Paul speaks also of all priests, including himself, as specially elected in the divine economy even before procreation and of all bishops and priests as chaste under the special protection of the Virgin Mary and continent for the sake of the kingdom (he alludes frequently to Matthew 19:12) and forever in that kingdom. Here he has in mind a global kingdom of divinely called and morally self-disciplined men and women who constitute a kind of *celibatocracy.* Although it is traditionally Catholic to think of the priest as called from his mother's womb, like Jeremiah (Jer. 1:5), and as retaining the indelible character of his ordination into eternity, John Paul, far from attenuating the distinction between the *sacerdotium* and the laity, stresses it; and in his address to seminarians in Nagasaki, Japan, on 25 February 1981 he spoke of "the Lord's seduction" of the prophet and priest (Jer. 20:7), of the priest's ordination as the climactic "anointment" of a "preferential love for a certain person" antecedent to procreation, and of consecration in the kingdom as being "forever."[25] On 8 April 1982 John Paul converted the customary Holy (Maundy) Thursday address to priests into an exhortative prayer, in which he derived the priesthood from Christ's "body and blood," "as a child

---

and Giroux, 1981), translation of the Polish original, *Miłość i odpowiedzialność: Studium etyczne,* 3rd ed., Serii niebieskiej Biblioteki polskiej, vol. 9 (London: Veritas, 1965). The first Polish edition was published at Lublin in 1960.

22. For a complete discussion of *Love and Responsibility,* see Williams, *The Mind of John Paul II,* pp. 151-63.

23. For an English translation of *Familiaris consortio,* see *L 'Osservatore Romano,* English ed., 21-28 December 1981, pp. 1-19. These topics are discussed again in "The Family, Contraception, Abortion: The Rights of Women as Mothers," a subsection of this essay's companion, "John Paul II's Relations with Non-Catholic States and Current Political Movements," *Journal of Church and State* 25 (Winter 1983). John Paul models conjugal life on the example of the Holy Family as amplified by the teachings of Jesus.

24. Cf. Williams, *The Mind of John Paul II,* pp. 288-96.

25. For John Paul's thought in general on this new ascetic ideal, see Williams, *The Mind of John Paul II,* pp. 104, 154, 288-305.

is born from its mother's womb.''[26] The pope, with his lofty conception of the ascetic ideal voluntarily entered into, in response to a
preordained vocation, firmly resists any devolution of the role of the
priestly ministry or any confusion of it with the equally emphasized
apostolate of the laity. This sacerdotal priesthood is made up of both
diocesan and religious priests and bishops, what were called in the
Middle Ages and long thereafter the secular clergy, serving in the
world, and the regular clergy of monastery or convent, monks and
friars.

The celibate men constituted collectively the *sacerdotium* during
the period of the Investiture Controversy, when Pope Gregory VII
(1073-84) and his successors sought to secure the universality of the
church by wresting its clergy, at least, from the particularization of
the feudal system. Gelasius I (492-96), in the context of the broken
Christian Empire, had declared, ''Duo quippe sunt''—''There are
two [orders] by which this world [*mundus*] is principally ruled—the
sacred authority [*auctoritas*] and the royal [i.e., imperial] power
[*potestas*].''[27] Under Charlemagne and his French and German
successors, royal and imperial, the *mundus* of the dictum of Gelasius
became *ecclesia*, in effect and often in formal asseverations; the
church is ruled by two: the king/emperor and the sacred power. In
the reforms of Gregory VII[28] the dictum of Gelasius was again
reworded; the world (Christendom) is ruled (indirectly) by the
church as *sacerdotium*, i.e., by the pope and the four higher celibate
orders of bishop, priest, deacon, and subdeacon, and directly by the
king/emperor. Under Innocent III (1198-1216),[29] Boniface VIII
(1294-1303), and the other thirteenth-century popes in between, the
sacred authority became almost imperial.

There not only survives in the pontificate of John Paul, but he has
expressly stated in many different ways the view that in some sense
there is a universal and international celibate *sacerdotium* working
closely in harmony with women who have similarly been called to a
life of service in and to Christ in the voluntary eschewing of
marriage.

John Paul connects the celibatocracy of chaste self-discipline not
only with the model of Christ but also in particular with the chastity

---

26.   The address/prayer was released on 1 April 1982 and appeared in *L 'Osservatore Romano*,
English ed., 19 April 1982, p. 6.
27.   Andreas Thiel, ed., *Epistolae Romanorum Pontificium*, 2 vols. (Braunschweig: E. Peter,
1868), 1:350 ff., author's translation.
28.   For the issue of a celibate clergy in Gregory VII, see Anne Llewellyn Barstow, *Married
Priests and the Reforming Papacy: The Eleventh-Century Debates* (New York: Edwin Mellen
Press, 1982).
29.   Cf. the comments below on Innocent III, at fn. 42.

of Mary. In his homily at the Marian shrine of Altötting in West Germany on 18 November 1980, he placed the celibacy of religious, male and female, in a Marian and an eschatological context. Approaching vehemence, he said:

[B]y the great yes of your life you have chosen consecrated celibacy "for the sake of the Kingdom" (Matt. 19:12). In this way you are a visible sign of the coming Kingdom of God. . . . Mary . . . carries the features of that woman whom the Apocalypse describes (Rev. 12:1) [as] "adorned with the sun, standing on the moon . . . ." The woman, who stands at the end of the history of creation [the proto-evangelium of Genesis 3:15] and salvation, corresponds evidently to the one about whom it is said . . . that she "is going to crush the head of the serpent." Between this promising beginning and the apocalyptic end Mary has brought to light a Son "who is to rule all nations with an iron sceptre" (Rev. 12:5).[30]

This international *sacerdotium* is the ninth meaning of *ecclesia*.

If, then, there is something like a celibatocracy or world communion of priests, secular and regular, under their highest counterpart, the *Summus Sacerdos*, the nuns and sisters under their superiors of various titles, there is also the control center of this celibatocracy which is the papacy itself understood collectively as the Vatican. At once there is a church and a state made up of the pope, the curia of cardinals heading sacred congregations, secretariats, dicasteries,[31] and the diplomatic corps.

NINE KINDS OF STATES AND JOHN PAUL'S VIEWS ON REDEMPTION, MERCY, WORK, THE FAMILY, PEACE, AND ECUMENISM

This subtitle is suggested by John Paul's first three encyclicals and by his assignment of a political status to the family, by his unprecedented involvement in peace initiatives, and by his still incompletely formulated view of intrafaith and interfaith ecumenism. Moreover, before becoming pope, Karol Wojtyla had read seriously in sociology and social theory and had indeed written, especially concerning the individual, on various social contexts. This prepapal thinking plausibly colors, if not wholly shapes, John Paul's papal utterances on church-state issues and his understanding of the kinds of states and variant social systems with which the papacy, national episcopal conferences, and local Catholic institutions (like universities and parochial schools) must relate themselves.

If under the *Pastor omnium* there are as many as nine possible meanings of church, from the Holy See to the quasi church of the

---

30. "Help Protect the Freedom of the Gift," *L'Osservatore Romano*, 19 November 1981, pp. 1, 3, author's translation.
31. For more on the dicasteries, see below, at fn. 44.

home confirmed in a new ascetic ideal, then, given the Slavic headship of the Catholic Church for the first time in history, clearly the problem of church and state in John Paul II takes on characteristics distinctive of his pontificate. These characteristics are related in part to his experiential, philosophical, and theological antecedents, in part to the radically altered postcolonial demographic and political situations with which John Paul is faced. He faces them no less than the World Council of Churches, which has been swiftly de-Europeanized to the advantage of churches in the Second and the Third World, and the North Atlantic community within the United Nations, where also the clamors, challenges, and sensibilities of the Third World are most urgently and incessantly voiced.

Karol Wojtyla has, from the beginning of his clerical career, been trained within the authoritarian context of the occupying Nazi authorities and of the ideologically Marxist People's Republic. For his second doctoral thesis, to qualify to teach in a university, he studied Max Scheler, a contemporary of Max Weber and Ernst Troeltsch, notably Scheler's *Der Formalismus*.[32] Scheler's work is replete with a theory of social togetherness: *Gesellschaft* (society), *Gemeinschaft* (community), *Genossenschaft* (fellowship), and other terms and concepts of an emerging sociology and sociology of religion. Wojtylan modifications of these terms in their Polish equivalents recur frequently. Wojtyla writes about society, about capitalistic, individualistic society ("individualism," "Utilitarianism," and "social egoism"), Marxist collectivism ("totalitarianism" and "totalism"), and ideal community and intimate communities ("I-thou communities" moving into "we-communities"). Although in his prepapal writings Wojtyla was well on his way to giving a distinctive meaning to these terms in sociology and sociology of religion, of which states of various ideologies and confessions of faith are reflections, he had shown the most analytical and then constructive interest in that kind of togetherness in which the sovereign person emerges, is sustained, and, by personal intention, freely transcends himself for the common good, namely, within the *Gemeinschaft/wspólnota/communio*, this last term in the sense both of sacramental communion and of I-thou-we-you intimacy and mutual concern.[33]

---

32. Max Scheler, *Der Formalismus in der Ethik und die materiale Wertethik*, 5th ed. (Bern: A. Francke, 1966), translated as *Formalism in Ethics and Nonformal Ethics of Values: A New Attempt Toward the Foundation of an Ethical Personalism*, trans. Manfred S. Frings and Roger L. Funk, Northwestern University Studies in Phenomenology and Existential Philosophy (Evanston, Ill.: Northwestern University Press, 1973). The first German edition was published at Halle in 1916 by M. Niemeyer.
33. See above, fn. 18. Cardinal Wojtyla dealt with these distinctions, as developed at Vatican

Wojtyla, in his communications about the social and therefore political and ecclesial aspects of collectivity, as philosopher-ethicist and now as pope, has thus tended to stress the primordial status of the sovereign person who, as he matures in the family and neighborhood, eventually, if normal, assumes ever greater responsibility and involves himself in an ever-widening range of "participation" (versus "alienation"). Wojtyla prefers to think in terms not of society or even of community and family as primordial; he thinks, rather, of diversified communities of responsible persons, of congeries of such communities eventually making up that entity of which the state is theoretically the sovereign expression. Although some of these communities can be egalitarian and only slightly hierarchical, he holds, of course, that the church as a supranatural community ordained of God is by nature hierarchical, although one enters the church (theoretically) voluntarily as a sovereign person.[34]

Apart from the church, John Paul is not only a personalist but also a sociocultural and even economic pluralist. Although he is temperamentally, and now also as pope *ex officio*, very political as well as pastoral, yet untrained in the canon law and papal diplomacy known so well by many of his predecessors, he has possibly a less firm theoretical grip on church-state theories than they; for even the major issue in this area on which he has written and spoken prepapally is again in the personal sphere of the liberty of conscience with respect to the state. Some of John Paul's impassioned appeals for peace are for an individual change of heart and remind one more of recent appeals from Billy Graham, now an opponent of nuclear war, than of John XXIII's socioinstitutional analysis of conflict in *Pacem in terris*.[35] Yet for all his theologically personalist and profoundly ethical concerns in extensive prepapal thought and writing, John Paul in his own incredibly keen observations of the global scene is bringing out "from the heritage of the Gospel 'what is new and what is old' [cf. Matt. 13:52],"[36] extraordinarily fresh insights and new

---

II, in addressing the Catholic University of Lublin in October 1960. His comments, accompanied by an authoritative French translation, appear as "Wspólnota ludzka w oczach Soboru," in *Zeszyty Naukowe*, nos. 1-3 (Lublin: Catholic University of Lublin, 1979), pp. 5-20, esp. pp. 11-12, 20.

34. For a similar view, see J. Brian Benestad, "The Political Vision of John Paul II: Justice through Faith and Culture," *Communio: International Catholic Review* 8 (Spring 1981):3-13.

35. For the Latin text of *Pacem in terris*, see *Acta Apostolicae Sedis* 55 (April 1963):257-304, available in English as *Encyclical Letter of His Holiness Pope John XXIII: Peace on Earth* (New York: Paulist Press, 1963).

36. Cf. also *Laborem exercens*, §2. For the Latin text of *Laborem exercens*, see *Acta Apostolicae Sedis* 73 (5 November 1981):577-647; for an English translation, see *Tablet* (London) 235 (26 September 1981):935-42, (3 October 1981):964-69. All subsequent references to *Laborem exercens* will appear in the text with the appropriate sections of the encyclical so designated.

guidelines in church-state relations.

As the pope works with some nine meanings of church, so by coincidence he may be said to work with roughly nine kinds of states and political or quasi-political entities in elaborating his theory and practice of church-state relationships, in building on the precedents of his predecessors within a global context. These are: the sovereign Vatican City itself and its diplomatic corps; the Republic of Italy, special because the pope is primate of Italy and because the republic and the Vatican have a special treaty and concordat governing the extraterritoriality of several enclaves; nonideological states, although some of these, like France and Mexico, might well trace their modern constitutions to revolutionary ideologies, and although some, like the United States and Mexico, with large or even prevailingly Catholic populations, have no diplomatic relations with the Holy See, while others, largely non-Christian, like Japan and Kuwait, have full diplomatic exchange; traditionally Christian states where either Orthodoxy (Greece), Lutheranism (Sweden), or Catholicism (Spain) has a preferred status but where freedom of religion, personal and corporate, is guaranteed by the constitution and upheld by public policy; non-Christian theocracies or states where one religion is official and Christian missions are forbidden or severely restricted; ideological states, mostly Marxist-Leninist, with often important or even prevailingly Christian populations, sometimes of various confessions, like Poland, Rumania, the USSR, Cuba, and Ethiopia, where the private exercise of religion is commonly constitutionally guaranteed but where individual believers and, to some extent, even within their precincts, the churches are under varying degrees of harassment; the state of Israel, which is nominally secular and which accords a quasi-official influence to Judaism and full religious autonomy to all non-Jewish religions, but which for various deep reasons constitutes a case almost as unique as Vatican City itself; infrastructural political entities, which include tribes with their own kings in several African states, regional governors, mayors, linguistic and ethnic minorities, dispossessed classes, political parties, organized labor, managerial capitalist organizations, and so forth; and finally, provisional or exiled governments or revolutionary cadres, like the PLO and the IRA.

It is not too early in John Paul's pontificate to discern what he thinks about the nine possible meanings of the term church or *ecclesia* and its sacerdotal authority, on whatever level, in relation to the nine forms and contexts of political power. In the perspective of almost two millennia of church history we can discern what seems to have emerged as the main outlines of what will come ever clearer into focus as John Paul approaches the third millennium.

The pope developed his papal thought about society and, indirectly, the role of the state in his third encyclical. Although the pope did not deal directly with church-state relations in *Laborem exercens*, its analysis of labor and capital in terms of "the dignity" and "spirituality of work" (§24), "the positive and creative, educational and meritorious character of man's work" (§11) constituted so profound a reworking of his own earlier meditations on work as to invite attention to the encyclical as one seeks to place John Paul's church-state thought on the economic-ideological global map.

Perhaps the first thing to note is that unlike Leo XIII's *Rerum novarum* on the condition of labor, of which it represents the ninetieth anniversary updating, *Laborem exercens* was addressed to Catholics and to all men and women of good will. Such an address had been true, of course, for John XXIII's *Pacem in terris*, since peace concerns all human beings; and such had also been true of John Paul's first encyclical, *Redemptor hominis*, even though its contents, while of broad human concern, presupposed in a central way Christian revelation. John Paul's second encyclical, *Dives in misericordia*, although dealing with the mercy of the God of all peoples, was addressed to Catholics. *Laborem exercens* was meant as a guide not only to the meaning of work but ultimately to the conflict between nations and ideologies based upon what the pope regarded as a false dichotomy between capital and labor. One is thus surprised when, on the quite specific requirement that a worker rest one day in seven and have other lengthier respites, the pope specifies Sunday as that weekly day of rest (§19). Even when he returns to this subject and says more generally that "man's work . . . requires a rest every 'seventh day'" (§25), it is in the context of the command in Genesis 2:2 and the commandment of rest among the Ten as modified by Christian usage in the observance of the commandment on the eighth day, that of the Resurrection. In this encyclical, meant surely to improve working conditions and the theology of work around the world, the pope could have put in parentheses at least some awareness of the Sabbath of Jews and of Sabbatarian Christians and the Friday of Moslems.

The fact is that *Laborem exercens*, dealing with the most fundamental activity common to all human beings, one distinguishing them from animals (although perhaps not with due appreciation for an animal's work, however "instinctive"), is built to an extraordinary degree not on natural law, prominent in *Rerum novarum*, but on scriptural revelation. In the Genesis revelation, hard work by the sweat of the brow for men and pain in childbirth for women were

intended as the respective punishments for the disobedience of
Adam and Eve (Gen. 3:16, 19). The pope mitigates the original
curse of work as toil "in the midst of many tensions, conflicts and
crises" (§§1, 19).[37] He concedes "the archaic way the saving thought"
was manifested (§11). Thus the encyclical, which takes Scripture far
more earnestly, especially in its literal sense as its primary religious
and ethical sense (cf. the classical Protestant reformers and modern
evangelicals), than did pre-Vatican II encyclicals, must be seen as a
profound Christian meditation on how in the fullness of time it is
indeed possible to speak of "the Gospel of work" (§§ 6, 7, 25, 26)
rather than the curse thereof.

The adult in his or her maturity, on the basis of the divine
injunction to subdue or dominate the earth (Gen. 1:27; §§ 4, 12) and
its natural resources, and as heir to the processed materials of gener-
ations and to the invented means of transportation and communication (§§ 13, 16), is "a part-owner of the great workbench at which he
is working with every one else" (§14). He finds sanction for the
dignity and spirituality of work in the fact that the faithful worker is
a cocreator with God (§7), likened by Jesus Christ to a vinedresser
(John 15:1) who "is working still" (John 5:15; §25), that Jesus
Christ was himself a carpenter and craftsman (§26), that many kinds
of toilers were lauded in the Old Testament (§26), and that Paul
enjoined work and set an example as a tentmaker. The pope adduces
Thomas Aquinas and others for good measure. The clarification of
work in terms of revelation and tradition should make every Christian rejoice in the freshness of the papal analysis, which contains
elements distinctly the author's long before he became pope,
although then as now there is only a trace of Martin Luther's
eminent contribution to the positive modern view of work in the
idea of the "secular" vocation (*Beruf*).

The encyclical is here set forth, however, not primarily for what it
says so freshly to Christians about work but rather for what it brings
to the attention of leaders in all communities of faith, in national and
international labor organizations, and especially in the great ideological blocs into which the world is economically and militarily
divided. Friedrich Engels and Karl Marx are expressly mentioned
(§11), not to be anathematized outright as the fathers of "collectivism" or "state capitalism," or of common, theoretical, and dialectical materialism, but as socioeconomic theorists who were seriously
deficient, despite their presumably good intentions, as were likewise

---

37. On the mitigation of the pain of childbirth, see the subsection "The Family, Contraception, Abortion: The Rights of Women as Mothers" in "John Paul II's Relations with
Non-Catholic States and Current Political Movements."

deficient the unnamed economic theorists of "liberalism," "the ideology" (§11) of " 'rigid' capitalism" and "neocapitalism." Advancing far beyond the problem of the working classes, the proletariat, and their emerging workmen's associations of *Rerum novarum*, John Paul extends the meaning of worker to include the bulk of adult citizenry and their labor—from coalmining to management, from scholarship to political administrations, from housekeeping, with its mothering, to computer-engineering.

Having fully enlarged the meaning of worker and of work itself by using Marx, who defined capital as "congealed work," the pope observes further that what "we have grown accustomed to calling *capital*" is made up of the natural resources of nature, "a gift, in the final analysis, by the Creator," and "the result of the historical heritage of human labor" on these resources and their successive processing and distribution (§12); he here and throughout uses all the terms of modern technology, from computer to telecommunication, and the educational institutions responsible for manning so complex an economy. Fundamental in all this is his refusal to accept as valid the subordination of the worker to work. Instead, he proclaims "the priority of labor over capital," "the primacy of man over things" (§12). He insists that his comprehensive view of work and of workers "overcomes the opposition between labor and capital" (§13).

Recognizing that both capitalism, however mitigated, and collectivism, however idealistically socialistic, lead in terms of common materialism, human selfishness, and pride to work which is nonparticipatory and alienating, the pope introduces the rather unusual distinction between indirect and direct employer. The former is, in effect, the whole system: "The concept of indirect employer includes both institutions of various kinds, and also collective labor contracts and the *principles* of conduct which are laid down by these persons and institutions and which determine the whole socioeconomic *system* or are its result" (§17). Within any variant of the two major rival systems in the world there are, of course, foremen, bosses, managers, planners, directors, and others.

It is thus the purpose of the pope in the encyclical, despite its Christian argumentation as to the dignity of work, to commend his practical proposals to responsible people in any system, to ease the tension between blocs and within societies and industries of every society, and to restrain the exploitation of underdeveloped, raw material-producing countries by supranational, multinational, or ideological combinations, indeed by any inordinate corporate economic power beyond appropriate international and national regulations. He intimates that the rigid capitalists and multinational managers, with their doctrinaire ideas about eminent domain of private ownership without heed to the common good in the exploitation of human and natural resources, can be ruthless to the citizens of their own countries and other countries in the pursuit of the company's good. Capitalist agents are not any less culpable (§4) than the collectivist bureaucrats and commissars, who, having collectivized the means of production for the good of the proletariat in what is more like state capitalism than socialism or ideal communism, "though not owning them, from the fact of exercising power in society, *manage* them [the common resources] on the level of the whole national or the local economy" (§§ 11, 14) and thus alienate persons and whole groups, as in capitalism.

It is useful to observe that the criticism of the two ideologies, liberalism (§11) and socialism seeking to become communism, and of the two resultant systems, capitalism and collectivism, is to be found, almost in the same words, in the prepapal writings of the pope, although the concepts have undergone significant elaboration in *Laborem exercens*, both as to the dignity and spirituality of work and to the invalidity of the capital-labor dichotomy in the ideologies of the two main contending systems. It is to be further noted that the pope has not given up confidence, as possibly Paul VI toward the end of his pontificate was disposed to do, in the capacity of the *Doctor omnium* to compose, on the basis of natural law and revelation, a teaching document on so generic and not specifically Christian an issue as work[38] with intended relevance in all parts of the world and for all conditions of men and even for confessions of faith beyond the Christian.

Yet, by suggesting that "unions do not have the character of political parties struggling for power" (§20), John Paul had the success of Solidarity so much in mind that he overlooked the structure and achievements of the Labour party in Great Britain and its counterparts elsewhere. At the same time, to a degree perhaps greater than he was aware, the pope had, in emphasis, replaced the

---

38. In a perceptive critique that places *Laborem exercens* in its historical setting, Peter Hebblethwaite, "Popes and Politics," *Daedalus* 11, no. 1 (Winter 1982):85-99, suggests that John Paul sought to revive, as universally valid, papal doctrine in line with Leo XIII's *Rerum novarum* while overlooking Paul VI's reluctant abandonment of such an effort. Hebblethwaite adduces Paul's 1971 letter to Maurice Cardinal Roy of Quebec, *Octagesima adveniens*: "In view of the varied situations in the world, it is difficult to give *one* teaching to cover them all or to offer a solution of universal value" (§4). This was a remarkable admission, coming as it did from the papal author of *Populorum progressio* (1967). Hebblethwaite holds that John Paul "deliberately set about the task of rehabilitating" a universal papal doctrine because he needs it to restrain liberation theology in the Third World and wishes to legitimize Solidarity in Poland and perhaps elsewhere in the Second World.

traditional Catholic protection of private property as sacrosanct; this he did by construing the person as inviolable regardless of his place in the organization of production and in all other kinds of work.

A key word in Catholic thought, especially since Pius XI, and very important in the theory and practice of John Paul II is "subsidiarity." Pius XI, in his encyclical *Quadragesimo anno*,[39] issued on 15 May 1931 on the fortieth anniversary of Leo XIII's *Rerum novarum*, gave currency to this term and concept that clarifies the level in society (whether at the personal or family level or all the way to the level of international law, or, in Catholic matters, to that of the pope himself) at which a given decision or issue—moral, economic, judgmental, political, theological—should be made or resolved. Pius XI's influential definition of subsidiarity was as follows: "[I]t is a fundamental principle of social philosophy, fixed and unchangeable, that one should not withdraw from individuals and commit to the community what they can accomplish by their own enterprise and industry. So, too, it is an injustice and at the same time a grave evil and a disturbance of right order to transfer to the larger and higher collectivity functions which can be performed and provided for by lesser and subordinate bodies" (§79). When in 1951 the archbishop of Dublin decisively opposed in Eire legislation for "the mother and child scheme" in imitation of the (Ernest) Bevin Plan in Great Britain, he appealed to the principle of subsidiarity, that the state should not intervene in family matters.[40] While the original Bevin Plan definition was indeed meant to enlarge the state's benign role in socioeconomic matters beyond its alleged competence for efficiency, subsidiarity in Catholic thought has everywhere, however, undergone an evolution in meaning in the last fifty years so that it becomes applicable to international and national polities, including the Catholic Church itself. In any case, it is a term and concept important for the socioeconomic and church-state thought and policy of John Paul II.

THE UNIQUENESS OF THE PAPACY

The order in which one should most appropriately take up the relationship, in the thought and policy of John Paul, between church in some nine senses and state and political entities in some

---

39. For the Latin text of *Quadragesimo anno*, see *Acta Apostolicae Sedis* 23 (1 June 1931):177-228; for an English translation, see *The Catholic Mind* 29 (8 June 1931):257-306. All subsequent references to *Quadragesimo anno* will appear in the text with the appropriate sections of the encyclical so designated.

40. See J. H. Whyte, *Church and State in Modern Ireland, 1923-1970* (Dublin: Gill and Macmillan, 1971), pp. 62-302.

nine possible classifications—in terms of ideology, constitution, and subsidiarity—baffles logician, historian, and legal theorist. In his pontificate thus far, John Paul, with respect to some of these relationships, has not yet displayed clear confirmation of, or marked departure from, the strategies and teachings of his predecessors. Clearly, however, a presentation of the unique status of the papacy (as a church-state) itself comes first, regardless of the degree to which a distinctive trend or thrust has thus far been detected under John Paul.

As pope, John Paul is at once the incumbent of the Holy [Apostolic] See,[41] Bishop of Rome, Vicar of Jesus Christ, Successor of the Prince of the Apostles, Supreme Pontiff of the Universal Church, Patriarch of the West, Primate of Italy, Archbishop and Metropolitan of the Province of Rome, Sovereign of the State of Vatican City, and Servant of the Servants of God. Although in his capacity as Bishop of Rome the pope has a cardinal vicar with a large staff, in the case of the Polish pope an extraordinary amount of time and energy has been spent, with protracted personal involvement, in discharging this office and the Italian primatial office. As Bishop of Rome, the pope's official residence is the Lateran Palace, an extraterritorial part of Vatican City State, along with Castel Gondolfo.

The title *Vicarius Christi* was once an imperial title that only in the pontificate of Innocent III definitively replaced the venerable *Vicarius Sancti Petri*, Successor of the Prince of the Apostles.[42] John Paul, who at Cracow was always proud of being the successor of martyred Saint Stanislaw (d. 1079), frequently calls himself the Successor of Saint Peter; he is noticeably sparing in his use of the title *Vicarius Christi*. Supreme Pontiff derives from *Pontifex Maximus*, the ancient pagan Roman title of Highest Priest, which was assumed by the first Roman emperors. The final official title of the pope, *Servus servorum Dei*, is one assumed by Gregory I (the Great, 590-604) to rebuke the patriarch of Constantinople for assuming the title carried to this day by his successors, Ecumenical [Universal] Patriarch, taken because his see was in the new capital (founded A.D. 330) of the Roman Empire. By 451 there were five patriarchs in the empire. "Ecumenical" for Constantinople (sixth century) at the least implied general oversight of Christians not under the other four patriarchs, especially beyond the empire to the north and east. The Patriarch of the

41. The nomenclature in this sentence is derived from *Annuario Pontefico, 1982* (Vatican City: Librería Editrice Vaticana, 1982), p. 27.
42. For a history of the pope's many titles and a general history of the papacy itself, see Friedrich Gontard, *The Chair of Peter: A History of the Papacy*, trans. A. J. Peeler and E. F. Peeler (New York: Holt, Rinehart and Winston, 1964).

West was destined after 1492 to become ever more "ecumenical" as the nations of Latin Christendom spread overseas their colonies and empires (whether Catholic or Protestant) and as their successor states of "Western" civilization flourished, at the zenith of colonialism, in virtually all areas except Korea, Japan, and China; the pope was Highest Pontiff *universae Ecclesiae* (a combination of titles consolidated by Vatican I). The title *Sovrano dello Stato* derives from the Lateran Pacts of 11 February 1929, which included a treaty between the pope as *Sovrano* of Vatican City State, with its two extraterritorial palaces and other rights, and the concordat annexed thereto between the Holy See and the Kingdom of Italy.

John Paul's actions as *Sovrano* are of special interest here. The pope had been, at the climax of the papacy's medieval development, *Verus Imperator* (a title taken by Innocent III), with plenitude of political as well as spiritual power. In post-Napoleonic Italy, however, the pope was simply head of state for one of some five major states in the peninsula and as such entitled to send diplomatic missions beyond the Papal States to other states on the peninsula and abroad and to receive emissaries. Because the papacy has so long been a temporal power with direct and indirect influence in the world or at least in Catholic states, another kind of purely ecclesiastical envoy was needed; the *apocrisiarius* and the *legatus a latere* (this latter office at once temporal and spiritual in the Middle Ages) atrophied, and the spiritual and temporal functions were combined in the *nuncio* and *internuncio* as the distinctive names for papal envoys. During one period when the papacy was an Italian territorial state, the United States, despite the American constitutional principle of church-state separation, had a minister accredited to the Holy See, first as chargé d'affaires (1848-55) and then as minister resident (1855-68). When, except for Rome and Venice, the Italian peninsula was politically united by 1861, France under Napoleon III still protected Rome from being absorbed. When French troops had to be withdrawn in the course of the Franco-Prussian War, Rome was declared the capital of the united Kingdom of Italy under Savoyard Victor Emmanuel on 1 July 1871. Thereupon the Holy See was bereft of any protective political carapace, although by the Law of Guarantees of 13 May 1871 the pope was secured in his possession of the Vatican and the Lateran and Gondolfo palaces, awarded an annual subsidy in lieu of direct compensation for lost territories, and above all accorded the unimpaired right to send papal envoys and to receive foreign ambassadors.

The "Roman Question," from the point of view of pope and curia, could not be so easily disposed of; after the expression of much bitterness, however, with the popes in succession deploring their status as "prisoners of the Vatican," they gradually recognized a spiritual advantage in the legalization of a diminutive *Stato della Città del Vaticano* in international law. The Lateran Pacts of 1929 provided that all bishops of Italy, except for the seven suburbicarian bishops who retained special relations with Vatican City State, should swear an oath of allegiance to the king on taking possession of their dioceses.

The title of Pope, while used by the patriarch of Alexandria and even in modified form by the ordinary priest in some Eastern traditions, was declared by Gregory VII, in his *Dictatus papae*, to belong uniquely to the Bishop of Rome. It is quite possible that in canon law, as in general Catholic usage, there is studied ambiguity concerning the distribution of the pope's titles with respect to this elective absolute monarch's authority in the two intersecting spheres, the spiritual Holy See and the temporal Vatican City State. Interestingly, ambassadors are accredited not to the Vatican but to the Holy See. When the Holy See is not recognized diplomatically by a non-Christian country, like China, or by a Catholic country, like Mexico, or a country with a large Catholic population, like the United States, the Holy See will nevertheless have in the capital of such states (where the principle of separation operates to inhibit formal diplomatic exchange) an apostolic delegate or, in the case of the U.N., an apostolic mission.

As for other titles, the pope is more likely to be called Holy Father by the Catholic faithful and His or Your Holiness by non-Catholics wishing to express respect. A term used with less frequency today than after the promulgation at Vatican I of *Pastor aeternus* on 18 July 1870, which defined the primacy, infallibility, and universal immediacy of the Bishop of Rome's episcopal jurisdiction, is *Omnium Christianorum Pastor et Doctor*. The pope is held to be pastor of the whole flock of Christ and, by virtue of the universalizing soteriology of Vatican II, teacher of all the children of men on the basis either of revelation, natural law, or Christ's universal intent in altering human nature through his renewed headship of the race as the Second Adam.[43]

Besides the pope,[44] there are his secretary of state; the prefects of the sacred congregations (the most important being the former Holy Office, since Vatican II renamed the Doctrine of the Faith);

---

43.   The title *Omnium Christianorum Pastor et Doctor* goes back at least to the Ecumenical Council of Florence in 1439.

44.   For descriptions of the political bodies that govern Vatican City, see Robert Neville, *The World of the Vatican* (New York: Harper and Row, 1963). See also above, fn. 31.

and the secretariats, headed by cardinal presidents and the various tribunals, which in the strict sense are the dicasteries. The last term is commonly used to cover congregations, secretariats, and tribunals. There are also offices, institutes, universities, and the cardinalitial commission for the governance of Vatican City, including a governor. In the secretary of state's evolution from one of several Renaissance secretaries in the literal sense, he should not be understood, since the unification of Italy, as primarily the first political minister of the pope and therefore as charged solely with diplomacy, but rather as the personage closest to the pope in dealing with the dicasteries and all other curial entities.

As compensation in 1929 for its lost territory, Vatican City received the equivalent then of $40 million in cash and $60 million in bonds of the new kingdom and thereby, under Italian popes, became inextricably bound in Italian party politics.[45] The Lateran Pacts were renegotiated and the provisions incorporated with only slight modification by the Republic of Italy in the constitution of 1 January 1948.

The basic internal revision of the Holy See and Vatican City took place under the impact of Vatican II with the apostolic constitution of Paul VI, *Regimini Ecclesiae Universae*,[46] issued on 15 August 1967, in which the evolution of the secretary of state as deputy of the pope in all papal functions was formally consolidated. In other words, John Paul's (second) cardinal secretary, Agostino Casaroli, should be thought of much less as minister of state than in the days of the Papal States, and, by the same token, the pope should be thought of as by no means disencumbered of temporal, international, and political matters. Indeed, John Paul II, already much more than Paul VI, acts the *Sovrano* and architect of diplomacy; he is served by a Spanish (rather than Italian) deputy secretary (*sostituto*), Archbishop Eduardo Martínez Samolo, who has ready access to the pope.

The Holy See, carapaced by Vatican City, is a global celibate bureaucracy, discharging a universal magisterium and jurisdiction. In this sense this church-state (the Holy See/Vatican) represents an approximation of perfection unique among temporal and religious societies, a universal *imperium Romanum ecclesiasticum* of the six

---

45. For a specialized study of this subject with related literature, see Jean-Guy Vaillancourt, *Papal Power: A Study of Vatican City Elites* (Berkeley: University of California Press, 1981); see also Francis X. Murphy, *The Papacy Today* (New York: Macmillan, 1981), a work which only goes through John Paul I but does find place to refer to John Paul II as "intensely political" while being otherworldly.

46. For the Latin text of *Regimini Ecclesiae Universae*, see *Acta Apostolicae Sedis* 59 (31 October 1967):885-928; for an English translation, see *The Catholic Mind* 65 (November 1967):43-65.

continents and of the seven seas.

As a prelate from a far country and people, one always loyal to Rome, even though the Vatican did little or nothing to support the aspirations of the Polish nation before and after the final tripartition in 1795, John Paul found in his minuscule state just that degree of symbolic sovereignty to free him as pope to serve the Catholic Church and the nations as a sovereign person. He is the one pontiff in the twentieth century not to have seen service in Vatican City or the secretariat of state before his election to the Apostolic See and has therefore fortunately absorbed none of the toxic residues in his psyche that long determined the melancholy or bellicose stances of popes and prefects from the dissolution of the Papal States to John XXIII. His predecessor of thirty-three days, John Paul I, had dispensed at his installation with the wearing of the papal tiara. John Paul II followed him in this[47] and abandoned the papal "we," although he will occasionally refer to himself in the third person as the pope, sometimes when most firm, often when most ingratiating and intimate in his public communications. In the four years of his pontificate John Paul does not appear yet to have constitutionally changed the Holy See or Vatican. He gave canonical status in Rome to the Pontifico Istituto Notre Dame of Jerusalem on 13 December 1978.[48] On 23 August 1982, making use of a Vatican II provision, John Paul became the first pope to elevate the headship of the Sacerdotal Society of the Holy Cross and Opus Dei into a "personal prelature," i.e., directly under him. Henceforth the head of the Society was to be like a general of an order, a ruler of a kind of international diocese (potentially free of immediate local episcopal supervision). He established the Institute for Polish Culture in 1980; on 20 May 1982 he also placed under the secretary of state the newly established Pontifical Council of Culture "for church-culture dialogue."

The New Code of Canon Law, worked on in the spirit of Vatican II by the late conservative Pericle Cardinal Felici, but necessarily revised for promulgation on 27 November 1982 under the impact of John Paul's clearly expressed views, excludes women, whether in religious orders or not, from serving as papal legates.[49] The theological and historical basis for the nonordination of women for service at the altar has been that the celebrant, taking the place of Jesus Christ at the Last Supper, reenacts the saving mystery of the Eucharist *in persona Christi*. Proponents of the ordination of women argue

---

47. Williams, *The Mind of John Paul II*, pp. 254, 257.
48. *Annuario Ponteficio, 1982*, the entire section entitled *Istituti*.
49. For information on the New Code of Canon Law, see above, fn. 7.

that the celebrant acts *in persona Ecclesiae* and can therefore be either male or female, since in the community of faith there is neither male nor female.[50] If the argument remains valid that the male priest at the altar acts *in persona Christi*, then a special urgency would seem to be given to the appointment of women to represent the Church in other respects, notably in diplomacy and in decision-making positions in the curial administration around the Church, which is indeed *Mater Ecclesia*. Yet the Code excludes women as legates and at most allows them to be commissioners. John Paul is, by the very force of his winsome personality, intercontinental visibility, and accessibility, changing the spirit of the papacy and the tone of the Vatican. It may be that one will presently descry the outlines of his ecclesiology as it illuminates the Holy See and the uniquely political Vatican City State. John Paul has not, however, suggested a reconception of his diplomatic corps along the radical lines once suggested by (now retired) Leo Jozef Cardinal Suenens.[51]

John Paul did take the bold step, however, of convening all cardinals in November 1980 to deliberate with him on finances, curial reform, and possibly the role of the Catholic Church in relation to culture. He may have been thinking of a recurrent gathering of the princes as an upper house of peers for the spiritual realm, while the largely elective synod of bishops already serves as the lower house, although it has in it many cardinals. Several bishops in the synod are there *ex officiis*, and 15 percent of the synod is approved by the reigning pope, the remaining deputies being elected by their national episcopal conferences. (Cardinal Wojtyla was elected or invited by the pope for the first five synods.)[52] Even as a cardinal and a member of the synod of bishops, however, Wojtyla opposed making that partly elective synod, representative of the world episcopate, anything but a consultative body designed to advise Paul VI, not to legislate, even on lesser matters, for the Church.[53] When he came to preside as pope at the sixth synod, unlike Paul VI, John Paul was present throughout, taking notes and raising questions. The findings of the synod he drafted as his apostolic exhortation, *Familiaris consortio*, in which differing views for presentation, as those authorized by the American episcopate on papal teaching concerning the family, served only in the end to articulate more cogently and explicitly the papal position.[54]

---

50. Williams, *The Mind of John Paul II*, p. 291, Cf. also Gal. 3:28.
51. Williams, *The Mind of John Paul II*, p. 227.
52. Ibid., pp. 182, 220-38, 253, 292.
53. Ibid., pp. 226-29.
54. See above, fn. 23. For reports on the twenty-seven congregations at the sixth synod, see issues of *L'Osservatore Romano* from 26 September 1980 to 3 November 1980.

It is an understandable anomaly of papal development that the Polish pope should still theologically fondle the three-tiered tiara which his namesake had renounced at his simplified installation. The tiara, with its three coronets once symbolic of papal control over the Church militant, expectant, and triumphant, has of fairly recent date been interpreted as symbolic of the *triplex munus Christi*, the threefold office of Jesus Christ as Prophet, Priest, and King.[55]

In the office of king John Paul is sovereign of Vatican City. In the office of priest he is *Pontifex Maximus*, the head of the dicasteries of the curia, convener of the synod of bishops, of the sacred college of cardinals, and, if the occasion should arise, of a council. Collegial with bishops, he as *Summus Sacerdos* has immediate power of jurisdiction in any see, should he choose. In the office of prophet he is teacher of the church and the nations, as the church herself is defined as *mater et magistra gentium;* he is *Doctor omnium*, authoritative in his ordinary magisterium, which can be exercised alone or in collegiality with the bishops; and, on occasion, he speaks infallibly *ex cathedra*.[56] In the exercise of his threefold office he is Vicar of Christ. Even with the tiara surviving functionally only on the papal coat of arms, the papacy today still involves the discharge of all three offices, and here is a convenient way of describing John Paul's conception of the Catholic Church as the Holy See/Vatican.

John Paul has defined several times his conception of the papacy, administratively and magistrally. On 3 April 1981, the fiftieth anniversary of the first Radio Vatican, erected by Marquis Guglielmo Marconi, he said to the Union of European Broadcasters:

[You] are guests . . . of a minuscule state, . . . minimal territorial expression of a sovereignty of which the principal purpose is to assure the full autonomy of exercise of a spiritual authority of the Holy See, center and heart of a pacific community of believers which knows not frontiers but which unites them all in one faith. The Apostolic See places itself above all diversity of ideology, but at the same time it nourishes, as it has always done, a profound respect for the grand variety of cultures in which the evangelical message incarnates itself among diverse peoples, and it is open to every form of fruitful collaboration with Christians of other confessions, with the believers of other great religions, and with men of good will.[57]

In other addresses to diplomats the pope has stressed the apostolic presence through nuncios and other envoys among the nations, as

---

55. The *triplex munus Christi*, though the formula had scriptural and patristic sources, began its modern career with Erasmus of Rotterdam, passing from him to the Reformed, particularly to the Polish Brethren, then to Anglicans, Lutherans, and eventually Catholics. For further comments, see Williams, *The Mind of John Paul II*, pp. 248, 298.
56. Williams, *The Mind of John Paul II*, pp. 248-49, 298, 310.
57. *L'Osservatore Romano*, 4 April 1981, pp. 1-2, author's translation.

they among diverse cultures ideally uphold "man as the supreme sovereign."

In a representative but metaphorically interesting annual address to the diplomatic corps accredited to the Holy See, he said: "All peoples should find themselves here because here is the house of all. The universal vocation of the Church concerns, in effect, each of the nations. . . . The diplomatic representatives accredited to the Holy See should not—even if they are not Catholic or Christian—feel themselves 'strangers' in the house of the universal pastor."[58] John Paul likes to think of each papal nuncio as taking the lead in serving as a model for every diplomat, desiring each to be "a builder of bridges between nations, to be a specialist in dialogue and understanding, to be a defender of human dignity and the common good," to be alert to "the economic and social disparities that exist in the world community," and hence to feel called upon to promote "the unity of the whole world" in "the North-South dialogue."[59]

In his pilgrimages (with two recent exceptions), which he expressly defines as "pastoral" to reinforce the faith and discipline of the bishops, priests, religious, and laity of the Roman Catholic Church, as well as to greet others, he seems nevertheless to have gone out of his way to act the sovereign no less than the pastor. He greets heads of state from over their airspace. He visits the political leaders of a country very near the beginning of his pastoral visitation, arriving, for example, in the interior capital of Brazil after a very long journey, rather than in Recife or Rio de Janeiro, precisely to signalize his coming as a sovereign, yet to proclaim his visit as preeminently pastoral. In his regular address to the diplomatic corps in every capital he has visited, he belies the claim that his visit is primarily pastoral. The only exceptions to his arrival on apostolic pilgrimage in a city other than the capital were in the United States and in Switzerland.

In the Republic of Ireland he landed at the smaller Dublin airfield rather than at Shannon International Airport; in Turkey at Ankara; in West Germany at Bonn; in the United Kingdom at London (on an expressly "ecumenical and pastoral" visit); in Argentina, despite the state of war, at Buenos Aires (and with the Argentinean president). One reason that he landed in Boston from Ireland on 1 October 1979 was to underscore the fact that a principal stated goal was to address the United Nations, a privilege accorded only a personage of state. He made Washington, therefore, his final stop.

---

58. *L'Osservatore Romano*, 12-13 January 1981, pp. 1-2, author's translation.
59. *L'Osservatore Romano*, 1-2 December 1980, pp. 1-2, author's translation.

The journey, however, to the United States was, of course, pastoral. The only journey John Paul has yet undertaken as *Sovrano* only was to Geneva to address the International Labor Organization on 15 June 1982, in token whereof he did not kneel to kiss the tarmac, as he would on a pastoral mission.

Since John Paul spoke in Geneva as *Doctor omnium*, here is a good place to note the double meaning of the prophetic office in the Judeo-Christian tradition, an office which in the fullness of time was integrated into the *triplex munus Christi*. For the most part, John Paul and his predecessors, insofar as they have recovered for pope and bishop the term *prophet*, make it roughly equivalent to the teaching office, the magisterium. John Paul, however, and especially some of the *periti*, who shaped some of the major documents at Vatican II, have given currency to the *triplex munus Christi* and also have fostered the devolution of these offices, in modified form, to the laity. Accordingly, the Catholic layperson is also a "prophet" and also endowed "with kingly power" in the home, at work, and in the parish as one who upholds received truth and who faithfully transmits it; as "sovereign over self," he "does not conform to the world" (Rom. 12:2). Yet in the Old Testament the prophet was often "no son of a prophet" (Amos 7:14), in any case generally a charismatic and an especially courageous critic of the society of the people in covenant, even of the anointed king and of the hereditary priests of the Temple. When Christianity became the established religion of the Roman Empire this prophetic office passed to bishops. Ambrose of Milan was specific about his being a Nathan rebuking a David, an Elijah rebuking Ahab and Jezebel, in the persons of Theodosius, Justina, and Valerian II. Saint Stanislaw, patron saint of Cracow and all Poland, was such a bishop rebuking King Boleslaw; Stanislaw is revered with special devotion by Pope Wojtyla.

Yet when Archbishop Oscar Romero, who has similarly discharged the office of social critic from the pulpit, was slain at a (hospital) mass on 25 March 1980, exactly like Saint Stanslaw, John Paul in his message of condolence to San Salvador deplored the depravity of the assassins but failed to note the discharge of the prophetic office in the Old Testament sense by this courageous convert to nonviolent support of rapid social change and justice;[60] this was in marked contrast to the way the pope had praised Saint Stanislaw the year before in *Rutilans agmen*, which contained clearly pointed communist analogues to King Boleslaw, who had killed the sainted bishop at mass.[61]

---

60. *L'Osservatore Romano*, English ed., 31 March 1980, p. 1.
61. For the Latin text of *Rutilans agmen*, promulgated on 8 May 1979, see *Acta Apostolicae*

John Paul's Dealings With Various Catholic States

It is appropriate next to take up John Paul's dealings with traditionally Catholic states. In some of these the Catholic Church and the state were hostilely separated, e.g., in France by the (Emile) Combes Laws of 1905 and in Mexico by violence toward the hierarchy through President Benito Pablo Juárez (1857-72) and by the nationalization of church property and the radical marginalization of even a native *sacerdotium* (priesthood and hierarchy) in the constitution of 1917.

No traditionally Catholic state has escaped turmoil and revolution, but some have entered the final quarter of this century largely intact and receptive to the evolving highest Catholic teaching with respect to church and state: the Republic of Ireland, Land Bayern (Bavaria), Austria, Italy, and even Poland, despite its communist government since 1944/45. Spain and Portugal, and most of the states that declared their independence of them, have in some cases only gradually, if not yet fully, come to comply with what would be regarded as normative for post-Vatican II Catholic concepts and practices with respect to church-state relations.

Because of the special relation of the Holy See with Italy and because he was from another country, John Paul at once began to make himself very much the bishop of Rome and the primate of Italy. He systematically visited Italian basilicas, churches, monasteries, shrines, and universities. He took as patrons of his own pontificate the two patrons of Italy, Saint Francis of Assisi and Saint Catherine of Siena. He has been indefatigable in his visitations throughout the republic, personally visiting and lamenting every major calamity and speaking at almost every possible commemoration. The most important fact is, however, that John Paul quietly dissociated himself from the Christian Democratic party in Italy[62] and Italian politics in general, except for taking specific stands as on the abortion referendum.

It was in connection with a banking scandal that John Paul has

---

Sedis 71 (31 July 1979):701-6; for an English translation, see *L'Osservatore Romano*, English ed., 28 May 1979, pp. 3 ff. See also John Paul's "St. Stanislaus—Witness in Catholic Poland," *L'Osservatore Romano*, English ed., 28 May 1979, pp. 3, 5, 11, a speech delivered 16 May 1979 that praises the martyred Polish bishop for precisely the same virtues as those displayed by Archbishop Romero.

62.   Observe the restraint in John Paul's tribute on 2 April 1981 to the founder of the Christian Democratic party, Alcide de Gasperi, at the centenary of his birth (*L'Osservatore Romano*, English ed., 2 April 1981, pp. 9 ff.) and the close reading of the pope's tribute found in Dominik Morawski, "Korespondencja z Rzymy," *Kultura* (Paris) 404, no. 5 (May 1981):19-24, esp. pp. 19-23.

been called upon to make most clear his understanding of Vatican City and the Republic of Italy. Lithuanian-American Paul C. Marcinkus, president of the Vatican bank since 1969, was elevated as archbishop by John Paul in 1980 and made propresident of the Pontifical Commission of Vatican City State. Archbishop Marcinkus wrote letters of support for Roberto Calvi, president of the Milanese Banco Ambrosiano, using Vatican assets as collateral. When on 18 June 1982 Calvi hanged himself from Blackfriars Bridge in London because of bankruptcy, the minister of the treasury of Italy proceeded on 2 July 1982 to investigate and asked the Vatican bank to cooperate. Although up to this point Archbishop Marcinkus had written and telephoned as an ordinary banker, John Paul suspended Marcinkus and asked a committee of three outside the Vatican to investigate while he also reminded the Italian government that, for its part, it would have to deal with the Vatican through its ambassador accredited to the Holy See and not through its minister of the treasury in its quest to uphold its strict banking laws.

The relations of John Paul with the nations of Iberia and Latin America necessarily have a special character. Personally drawn to the Carmelite tradition,[63] he wrote his first doctoral dissertation on the Spanish Discalced Carmelite Saint John of the Cross, whose mystical poetry and disquisitions on his own ecstatic poetry obliged Wojtyla to make Spanish the fourth of the many modern languages he has come to acquire.[64] The Iberian church-state legacy is distinctive. In the reconquest of the Iberian peninsula from the Moors, which climaxed in the expulsion of both Moors and Jews in 1492, Christian institutions had, more than elsewhere, the traits of an Islamic religio-political system. While the system was one which Catholic Iberians had long opposed, its traits became integral to their national character. Islam never clearly distinguished between "church" and "state," as Christianity had done in antiquity and as Catholicism had reformulated in theory and usage during the Investiture Controversy and reiterated much more fully in the post-Vatican II era.

Lay, sometimes royal, patronage, developed first in Portugal and then elsewhere on the peninsula, where it acquired distinctively Iberian traits. In Portugal the *padrõado* arose unobtrusively in 1319

---

63. Williams, *The Mind of John Paul II*, pp. 40-42, 75-81, 170-71. See also George Huntston Williams, "Teresian Carmelite Strains in the Personality of John Paul II," Address at the Carmelite Monastery, Boston, Mass., 12 September 1982.
64. Perhaps John Paul's most spectacular linguistic achievement was with Japanese, in which he said mass and delivered a homily while in Japan.

when the supressed Order of the Knights Templar was replaced by the Order of Christ for the purpose of propagating the faith among the heathen. The administrators of the Order of Christ were all members of the royal family. In effect, royal patronage (Spanish, *patronato real*) came to mean the royal appointment of bishops and other prelates, notably over the vast realms that came under the sway of Portugal and Spain after 1492. *Patronato real* was eventually claimed as a right by several of the states that had established their independence, notably Argentina, Bolivia, Ecuador, and Paraguay. This right is called *patronato nacional* and has a highly developed canonical, constitutional, and theoretical tradition, especially in Argentina.[65]

In this century, *patronato nacional* was exercised in Spain itself, as stipulated in the concordat, by Francisco Bahomanda Franco, who nominated half of the bishops of Spain. By 27 August 1953 a new concordat somewhat lessened Franco's control over the Church, a state of affairs which slowly evolved toward greater freedom for Spanish bishops. For non-Catholics the situation was most restrictive. The concordat held that Catholicism "continues to be the only religion of the Spanish nation" and "will enjoy official protection," although no citizen could be molested because of his beliefs; however, "the *public* cult of other religious denominations was not allowed."[66] In the constitution of 17 July 1967 the principle of religious freedom was incorporated under pressure from bishops who sought to implement the decrees of Vatican II.[67] After the death of Franco on 20 November 1975, with the Agreement (*Accordo/Acuerdo*) of Paul VI on 28 July 1976, established under King Juan Carlos I, there is an almost enthusiastic expression of compliance with the spirit of Vatican II in the acknowledgment that, while the Catholic Church has a special place in the life of the nation, the freedom of religion in the Decree of Religious Liberty is affirmed as properly a part of the Spanish constitution and as welcome to the Holy See and the Spanish signatory. The *Accordo/Acuerdo* of this date goes on in article one to bring *patronato nacional* to an end: "The naming of the archbishops and bishops is exclusively within the competence of the Holy See."[68]

John Paul's style is clearly evident in the *Conventiones* between the

---

65.· For John Paul's relations with Argentina, see below.

66.   For the Italian and Spanish texts of the concordat, see "Inter Sanctam Sedem et Hispaniam sollemnes conventiones," *Acta Apostolicae Sedis* 45 (27 October 1953):625-56; the quotations are the author's translations.

67.   For the text of this Spanish constitution, see *The Spanish Constitution: Fundamental Laws of the State* (Madrid: Ministerio de Información y Turismo, 1972).

68.   *Acta Apostolicae Sedis* 68 (31 August 1976):509-12, author's translation.

Holy See and Spain of 3 January 1979, signed for the Holy See by the same secretary of state who had signed the *Accordo/Acuerdo* of 1976, Jean Cardinal Villot.[69] This new and fuller agreement spells out in detail the place of the Spanish Episcopal Conference, that of Catholic universities, that of chaplains in the armed forces and the ecclesiastical independence of the chief of chaplains, the immunity of seminarians and priests from direct combat, and so forth. It deals thus almost wholly with the Catholic Church, as indeed any concordat would normally do; for whatever the reasons, however, the references to the dignity of the person in the Spanish constitution and the acknowledgment of the other confessions, so prominent in 1976, is limited to "the safeguarding of religious liberty of persons," presumably Catholic and non-Catholic.[70] John Paul's visit to Spain came on the 490th anniversary of the discovery of the New World. The pope's speeches and homilies in honor of Spain's role in world history and of Saint Teresa of Avila in the realm of the spirit all attest to the Polish pope's special feeling for Iberian spirituality and religious institutions, as well as for the general dignity of persons.

Here some observations should be made about John Paul's policy toward the states of Greater Iberia, from Angola to former Goa, from Portugal to the Philippines, from Abyssinia (once conquered by Portugal, hence the Uniate Ethiopian Church, with its college within Vatican City) to Argentina. With comments on the pope's trip to Mexico in 1979 and to Brazil in 1980 appearing elsewhere,[71] perhaps here a more general observation may be in order. Because of the history of the *patronato real* and *nacional* in Greater Iberia, it was inevitable that modern popes would seek to deal, at least in Latin America, with one ecclesiastical unit, in the hope of giving guidance to these disparate nations of but two principal languages in various stages of social and political development and relapse. Accordingly, Pius XII on 2 November 1955 laid the basis of what would be the *Consejo episcopal Latinoamericana* (CELAM), with its headquarters in Bogotá, Columbia. This council meets, however, only at the call of the pope, and it was John Paul I who had convened the 1978 council at Puebla in Mexico. In the end, in his first papal pilgrimage abroad, John Paul II managed to attend Puebla amid triumph everywhere in "anticlerical" Mexico, where religious habits in

---

69.   For the text of the *Conventiones*, see "Conventiones inter Apostolicam Sedem et nationem Hispanium," *Acta Apostolicae Sedis* 72 (31 January 1980):29-62.
70.   See "Conventiones inter Apostolicam Sedem et nationem Hispanium," art. 1, sec. 4, par. 2; art. 2, sec. 14.
71.   Concerning Mexico, see Williams, *The Mind of John Paul II*, pp. 263, 286, 326, 332; concerning Brazil, see Williams, *The Mind of John Paul II*, pp. 286, 318, 326.

public are still prohibited. Overcoming the restraint which he showed in Mexico in his utterances about liberation theology, John Paul was more open to this theology in Brazil. His stance must be seen in the context of the long history of the *patronato nacional* and indeed its appropriation, in modified form, by great Catholic landowners to justify their control of the peons and by Catholic entrepreneurs to legitimate their opposition to strikes by city workers.

The *patronato* extended in republican form to dictatorial President Ferdinand Marcos and his own Isabel, Imelda Marcos. Possibly the best example of how the pope conducts himself critically as well as benignly in an Iberian setting was his visit to the Republic of the Philippines, 17-22 February 1981, the only predominantly Catholic country in Asia. Although the republic has a large Moslem minority on the island of Mindanao, many Protestant churches, and the Aglipayan National Catholic schism of married priests (originated in 1902; from this tradition President Marcos originally came), the young sprawling state is overwhelmingly Catholic, and the Church is indigenized. The pope said in the presence of President Marcos in reference to the denial of civil rights "in exceptional situations": "Legimate concern for the security of a nation, as demanded by the common good, could lead to the temptation of subjugating to the state the human being and his or her dignity and rights."[72] John Paul refused, in a country where the Catholic Church, despite the strict separation imposed by the United States from 1898 to 1946, preserves some of the trappings and popular impulses of the Spanish *patronato real*, to occupy the special residence erected for him by First Lady Imelda Marcos; he was visibly annoyed by her repeatedly flying ahead of him and conspicuously kissing his hand in reverence in the presence of the assembled throngs at his several stops. She is governor of Metro Manila, a huge territory of several cities and towns, and also minister of populations and resettlements in the central government. John Paul in his role as sovereign was more than annoyed, for it seems to be his policy not to deal directly or very often by name with infranational semisovereigns or representatives of important internal jurisdictions, like ministers of state, governors, and mayors (except in Italy).

John Paul made a special effort to reach the hearts of the Moslems, then in murderous conflict with Catholics; he urged upon all, as citizens of a republic of islands, that, in the words of John Donne, "no one can be an island unto himself" and that all religious groups

---

72. *L'Osservatore Romano,* 18 February 1981, p. 2; John Paul II, *The Pope to the Filipino People* (Metro Manila: St. Paul, 1981), p. 28.

and social classes should work for the common good.[73]

Recently, during the suddenly conceded visit of the pope to Argentina, then in conflict with Great Britain, he made a bold address from the balcony of the Casa Rosada (from which, on 2 April 1982, President and General of the Armies Leopoldo Galtieri had announced the occupation of the Malvinas), saying: "There [in the South Atlantic] humanity should question itself, once more, about the absurd and always unfair phenomenon of war, on whose stage of death and pain only remain standing the negotiating table that could and should have prevented it."[74] He constantly asked for prayers of peace and for mercy for the fallen, wounded, and bereaved on both sides of the conflict.

The cry went up from many in Argentina on several occasions: "We want peace." Some chanted, "Juan Pablo, Peron, un solo corazón" ("John Paul and [Juan] Peron: one of heart"). It will be recalled that Peron had espoused the cause of the shirtless proletariat (*descamisados*) and had taken from their class his second and now almost sainted wife, Evita. Amid angry tumults he fell in 1955. Peronistas sacked and burned four churches in the capital and destroyed the episcopal curia and archives. In 1974 Peron returned from exile in Spain as caudillo, with his third wife, Isabel, his vice-president, who succeeded him at his death in the same year. The chiefs of the three military services seized power from her, placing her in internal exile, and waged war on various alleged and actual leftists of Cuban- or Chilean-Marxist sympathies, on armed Peronists called Mononeros, on other opponents of military rule, and on those supporting the rights of the poor, among these many young idealists, some of them not even Argentinean nationals. Up to fifteen thousand of these young people have disappeared without any record; they are the *desaparecidos*. The military government was forced to tolerate a weekly march and vigil of the white-kerchiefed "madres de la Plaza de [25] Mayo," the plaza being the monumental square commemorating the independence of Argentina (the United Provinces of Rio de la Plata) from Spain in 1816. On his way by train to the national Marian shrine at Luján, the pope waved, whether by chance or discretion, to the throng opposite of where, along the tracks, the Mothers of the Disappeared had assembled. In all his sermons, however, he stressed international and also social reconciliation; certain phrases about wounds and tensions in the body politic could be construed as allusions to violence before the war over the

---

73. *L'Osservatore Romano*, 21 February 1981, p. 2; John Paul II, *The Pope to the Filipino People*, p. 107.
74. "Excerpts from the Pope's Remarks," *New York Times*, Late ed., 12 June 1982, p. A4.

Malvinas. John Paul also intimated that the Argentineans would have peace when they had respect for all fellow countrymen. At Luján, where the Virgin had been accorded the honorary rank of captain-general of the Argentinean armed forces, he addressed her always as the Mother of Peace. As for the popular chanting identification of Juan Pablo with Juan Peron, the pope could not take cognizance of this passionate church-state idolatry, nor was the chant reported in the local press.[75]

While in Buenos Aires the pope telephoned the president of Chile; and although he promised to visit Argentina again and also Chile, John Paul reportedly would do that only after both countries (he meant primarily Argentina) had accepted the mutually requested and completed arbitrament of the territorial dispute between the two countries.[76]

One final event reveals much about John Paul's position concerning church-state relations. When the pope announced in November 1982 his intention to make a pilgrimage to the predominantly Catholic countries of Central America in 1983, he insisted as a condition of his visiting Nicaragua that all five priestly members of the government, including the foreign minister and the minister of culture, would have to resign.

For John Paul's relations with traditionally Catholic countries without the special Iberian idea of patronage, there remain of special interest Ireland, which he visited in September and October 1979, and France, which he visited in May and June 1980. In Ireland he was most outspoken against confessional violence or social violence allegedly sanctioned by religion. Although France is counted among the traditionally Catholic countries, a succession of revolutions has separated the Catholic Church from the state. Modern France is not so much, however, an example of separationism as of secularism. Still, in that part of France ceded by Germany at the end of World War I, Alsace and Lorraine, and recovered after World War II, the concordat with the Second Reich still upholds the Catholic Church, permitting some taxation for the church of one's choice and the maintenance of two theology faculties at the University of Strasbourg. Valéry Giscard d'Estaing was president of France

---

75. *La Prensa*, 12 June 1982, pp. 1, 4-9; *La Prensa*, 13 June 1982, pp. 1, 3-7; *New York Times*, Late ed., 13 June 1982, sec. 1, p. 28; *Newsweek*, 21 June 1982, p. 48; *L'Osservatore Romano*, 13 June 1982, pp. 1-2, 4; *L'Osservatore Romano*, 14-15 June 1982, pp. 1-3.
76. Concerning the papal arbitrament, see *Acta Apostolicae Sedis* 61 (15 January 1979):71; *L'Osservatore Romano*, English ed., 12 February 1979, p. 10; *L'Osservatore Romano*, English ed., 12 November 1979, p. 14; *L'Osservatore Romano*, English ed., 29 December 1980, pp. 2 ff. Cf. also various pronouncements on the Argentinean-Chilean conflict in *Acta Apostolicae Sedis* beginning 11 December 1978, the date papal arbitration was first requested.

when John Paul visited Paris. President Giscard d'Estaing showed none of the feelings that had once created the Combes Laws of church-state separation and hence necessitated the independent *instituts Catholiques* as separate faculties of theology, the most notable being near the Sorbonne. The president took the lead in welcoming the pope to the capital of what John Paul still wistfully called "the eldest daughter of the Church."

The most interesting expression of theory and policy with respect to a traditionally Catholic country, however, is that of the pope's dealings with his native Poland. This subject, however, is best considered under the broader heading of John Paul's policies toward and relations with non-Catholic states and current political movements.

John Paul II's Relations with Non-Catholic States and Current Political Movements

GEORGE HUNTSTON WILLIAMS

In a previous essay, "John Paul II's Concepts of Church, State, and Society," distinctions were made between some nine concepts of the meaning of *ecclesia* in post-Vatican II Catholic thought and some nine kinds of states.[1] One of these distinctions, unique in each series of nine, was the Holy See carapaced by Vatican City State, dealt with there, as was also John Paul II's relations with traditional Catholic states. Not all the remaining permutations of possible church-state relations will be dealt with in what follows. Rather, a delineation or analysis will be given of John Paul's views where these views have in the last four years been clearly expressed or significantly adumbrated on the Church with special reference, first, to various kinds of non-Catholic states around the world and, second, either to international and supranational political or quasi-political entities, such as the United Nations, or to infranational political entities, like regional governors, and quasi-political entities, like families, political parties, and labor unions, all of which, while they exist in national societies, can be treated by him in generic terms. Such issues as abortion, the right to strike, and civil liberties in general, all having ecclesio-political importance, come appropriately under this heading.

GEORGE HUNTSTON WILLIAMS (A.B., St. Lawrence University; B.D., Meadville Theological School, University of Chicago Divinity School; Th.D., Union Theological Seminary) is Hollis Professor of Divinity Emeritus, Harvard University, Cambridge, Massachusetts. Author and editor of many books including *The Radical Reformation* (1962), *Thomas Hooker: Writings in England and Holland, 1626-1633* (1975), *The Polish Brethren, 1601-1685* (2 vols., 1980), and *The Mind of John Paul II: Origins of His Thought and Action* (1981), his articles have appeared in *Archive for Reformation History, Church History, Harvard College Library Bulletin, Harvard Theological Review, Journal of Church and State, Mennonite Quarterly Review,* and others.

1. Although complementing an earlier article (George Huntston Williams, "John Paul II's Concepts of Church, State, and Society," *Journal of Church and State* 24 [Autumn 1982]:463-96), the present essay has its own integrity in treating John Paul's church-state policy as it unfolded into the fifth year of his pontificate. For the nine meanings of *ecclesia* and the nine kinds of states, see Williams, "John Paul II's Concepts of Church, State, and Society," §§1-3.

THE POPE AND NON-CATHOLIC STATES

By depoliticizing priests and nuns in the First and Third World, limiting their activity to the proclamation of justice, human rights, and human dignity in general terms without specific espousal of any local programs, parties, or revolutionary thrusts, John Paul evidently hopes eventually to be able to commend the Roman Catholic Church to the regimes of the Second World. This commendation is perhaps easiest to accomplish in his native Poland and most difficult in the USSR, where he has a concern for the future of perhaps 2.5 million Poles beyond the present Polish boundaries, for other Catholics in the three Soviet Baltic Republics (especially in Lithuania), and indirectly possibly for the Byzantine-rite crypto-Uniates of the Ukraine.[2] The crypto-Uniates still constitute a lively exarchy with a regional synod in which perhaps private feelings for the pope may be discretely expressed. The pope is also interested in the future of the Russian Orthodox Church itself. There is no doubt but that the Polish pontiff in Vatican City, who speaks Russian well, regards himself as in preparatory dialogue with the Kremlin.

On such an issue as the August 1980 boycott of the Olympic Games in Moscow, urged by President Jimmy Carter because of the Soviet invasion of Afghanistan, the sportsman pope was glad to make a positive gesture of solidarity among athletes and thus to be reckoned as nonaligned on a lesser First-Second World issue, one not directly pertaining to Europe.

The pope was personally represented at the funeral of Leonid Brezhnev, on 15 November 1982, by a member of the Pontifical Academy of Sciences and a member of the Pontifical Justice and Peace Commission. This remarkable gesture and the preceding telegram of condolence were all the more noteworthy because of the so-called Bulgarian connection that could implicate Brezhnev's successor, Yuri Andropov, with the attempt on the pope's life. Already in September, in the United States, a National Broadcasting Corporation (NBC) news team headed by Marvin Kalb had tracked down a relationship between the Bulgarian Secret Police (DS) and the attempt on the pope's life, which occurred on 13 May 1981. The head of the Soviet KGB in May, with close oversight in Bulgaria, was Andropov; further disclosures from the would-be assassin, Ali Agca, were being given

---

2.   After their dissolution by the forced Sobor of L'viv in 1946, the crypto-Uniates were obliged to renounce Rome and to come under the patriarch of Moscow.

prominence just as the reins of power at the Kremlin came into Andropov's hands.[3]

John Paul is concerned with Catholics in other communist countries not of the Soviet bloc (i.e., countries as far distant as Angola, with a new cardinal, and Vietnam), notably with the estimated 2.5 million Chinese Catholics who have declared themselves independent of the Holy See. John Paul's interest in regaining the allegiance of Chinese Catholics and of eventually visiting "your immense land" was so great that he addressed them while talking nominally to Filipino Catholics of Chinese extraction in Manila amid speculation that as a sovereign he might break off diplomatic relations with Taiwan in order to be supreme pastor over a body of former Catholics who are temporarily resisting allegiance to a "foreign" authority. He went so far in this February 1981 speech, meant to be reconciliatory with the Chinese government, as to declare all of China to be under Mary as Queen.

During the past several decades major developments had occurred in relations between Peking and Rome. National Catholic Bishop Michael Fu Tieshan of Peking had argued that even by 1950 only 20 of 143 bishops in the Chinese Church were Chinese and that during the war in Korea the Vatican had allegedly given orders "not to be patriotic."[4] The National Asso-

---

3. One must note the coincidence of the anticipated imminent death of Primate Wyszyński from cancer, which finally occurred on 28 May 1981, and the earlier attempt on the pope, which occurred on 13 May 1981. For reservations, however, about the facile attribution of the crime to Andropov and his superior, Brezhnev, see *Le Monde*, 3 December 1982, p. 22; Diana Johnstone, "The Bulgarian Connection," *In These Times*, 12-18 January 1983, p. 9; and Tass Dispatch, 29 December 1982. Tass quotes a party monthly, *Politicheskoe Samoobrazanie*, no. 12: "The pope has taken a much more conservative and rigid position vis-à-vis the socialist world," supporting the "notorious Solidarity" (author's translation). This observation was adduced in *Wall Street Journal*, 5 January 1983, sec. 1, p. 20, and by Smith Hempstone in *Washington Times*, 17 January 1983, p. 11A, as further evidence of Soviet complicity. The Tass observation might be sheer bravado in the face of accusations, or it might be evidence to the contrary. For CIA reservations as to the involvement of Andropov, see *Los Angeles Times*, 30 January 1983, p. 1; see also Henry Kamm, "Plot on Pope Aside," *New York Times*, Late ed., 28 January 1983, p. 1.

4. *L'Osservatore Romano*, 18 February 1981, p. 2; *L'Osservatore Romano*, 19 February 1981, p. 5; John Paul II, *The Pope to the Filipino People* (Metro Manila: St. Paul, 1981), p. 70. See also Williams, "John Paul II's Concepts of Church, State, and Society," at fn. 72. The pope appealed in this address (§3) to five main virtues: charity, justice, temperance, prudence, and fidelity; cf. the Panchisila of the 1955 Bandung Conference in Indonesia. These "constant virtues" appear in two versions: in terms of the older Confucianist school and, more fully by a later commentator, in terms of family virtue—humanity or love for neighbor (love of the mother), righteousness (associated with the father), propriety or ceremony-mindedness (fidelity), wisdom, and faithfulness or trust. See also George Huntston Williams, *The Mind of John Paul II: Origins of His Thought and Action* (New York: Seabury Press, 1981), p. 374, fn. 7.

ciation of Patriotic Catholics, formed by the government, was condemned by Pius XII in 1958.[5] This group adheres to the movement of the Three Selfs (for Catholics and Protestants) of self-support, self-evangelization, and self-government—no foreign help or control. Unaffected by Vatican II, the "native" Catholic Church still uses the Tridentine mass, and men and women generally worship in separate aisles. The one change was the permission of the priests to marry. In 1980, as a gesture of good will, Bishop Dominic Teng, S.J., of Canton, imprisoned for a score of years as a "counterrevolutionary," was released. He flew from Hong Kong to Rome and was consecrated archbishop of Peking by John Paul. In China the followers of Teng and hence of the pope may number a half million as they seek to implement the decrees of Vatican II and to indigenize the mass. When the pope spoke to China from Manila, he knew that already Bishop Fu Tieshan and two other national Catholics had attended, with seven Protestants from China, an ecumenical encounter in October 1981 with Canadian Christians in Montreal. Some small progress in mutual understanding had been accomplished as national Catholics for virtually the first time had an opportunity to converse with Vatican II Catholics as well as with Protestants, and with the approval of their government.[6]

Not long thereafter, in his 6 January 1982 letter to all bishops of the world, John Paul spoke of "hard suffering," of "difficult and prolonged trials," experienced by Catholics in China over the preceding thirty years, these comparable to the sufferings endured "by previous centuries of the Church," whose members had nevertheless "managed [like Dominic Teng] to remain faithful to the Holy See." Without acknowledging some minor concessions made since 1979 to the Chinese Catholics loyal to Rome, the pope besought the prayers of the bishops and the

---

5. Pius excommunicated the "patriotic" bishops in his 1958 encyclical, *Ad apostolorum principis*. For the Latin text of the encyclical see *Acta Apostolicae Sedis* 50 (September 1958):601-14; for an English translation, see *Catholic Messenger* 75 (25 September 1958):4.
6. Franz Cardinal König, "My Journey [by Invitation] to China," *Religion in Communist Lands* 8 (Winter 1980):268-73; Donald MacInnis, "Religious Revival in China," *Christian Century* 98 (1 April 1981):346-50; David Tracy, "Some Reflections on Christianity in China," *Criterion* 21 (Spring 1982):19-20; Christopher Lind, "China's Churches and the West," *The Ecumenist* 20 (March-April 1982):33-38. For the most recent conciliatory remarks of the pope predicting "ease" between the national community of China and Catholics there, see *L'Osservatore Romano*, 25-26 October 1982, p. 2. These remarks were made on 25 October 1982, the fourth centenary of the arrival in China of Matteo Ricci, S.J.

faithful for their cobelievers in China.[7] During the Angelus of 21 March 1982 the pope prayed, "through the intercession of Mary, Mother of China," that Catholics in China faithful to Rome be permitted to "live their faith, remaining in the Catholic unity of Christ's Holy Church," although the pope now added his expression of prayerful hope for general social progress for the whole of China.[8] On hearing this Angelus message broadcast through Vatican Radio Veritas in Manila, the National Association of Patriotic Catholics meeting in Shanghai denounced the message as containing "vicious slander"; and, denying the papal charges of persecution, the association gave its support to the punishment meted out "to the handful of scum [Vaticanists] of the Chinese Catholic community who have brought calamity to the country and the [official] Chinese Church."[9] Given the fact, well known by Sinologists (whether specialists in the Ming dynasty or Chairman Mao's successors), that the Chinese, even as Marxists, find universality beyond the Middle Kingdom hard to grasp conceptually, one might have thought that the diplomatically sophisticated pope could have found a formula bringing together the nationalist or "anglican" or "aglipayan" Chinese Catholics, who did have some grievance after the withdrawal of Chiang Kai-shek. The pope could have temporized or accommodated their positions, as he seems to be able to do in oppressively cruel parts of the world, where, as in Argentina, Chile, and the Philippines, martial law has taken many more lives than it has in his native Poland, if not in Mao's China.

In dealing with states of the Soviet ideological bloc, John Paul II, whose entire career as professor of philosophical ethics, as bishop and archbishop, and as cardinal had been devoted to establishing the right of Catholic citizens to participate in the political, economic, and cultural life of their nation, as pope seems wary about unduly arousing the anxieties of the rulers in the Kremlin, placing his hope for peace in a consolidation of Europe. While pursuing Paul VI's policy of *Ostpolitik*,[10] he has

---

7. *L'Osservatore Romano*, 24 January 1982, pp. 1-2, author's translation. See also *L'Osservatore Romano*, English ed., 1 February 1982, p. 9.
8. *L'Osservatore Romano*, 22-23 March 1982, p. 1, author's translation. For a complete English translation, see *L'Osservatore Romano*, English ed., 29 March 1982, p. 10.
9. Official Xinhua News Agency report, 23 March 1982; see also *New York Times*, Late ed., 24 March 1982, p. A7.
10. Concerning the evolution of this complex German term, see Williams, *The Mind of John Paul II*, pp. 12, 14, 230-32. On the recent history of the situation in Poland up to the election of Cardinal Wojtyla as pope, see Thomas E. Bird and Mieczyslaw Maneli,

Library of
Davidson College

concentrated on the perfection of acceptable concordats with various states in the Soviet sphere (those for Poland and Hungary are already in final draft) with a view to gaining full legal status for the Church in all these countries. It is his hope further that with the restoration of détente the once Latin-rite nations will be permitted to participate fully and freely in the Council of the Episcopal Conferences of Europe, which began informally in March 1971 in fulfillment of the Vatican II decree on the pastoral office of bishops, *Christus Dominus*.[11] The council received full canonical status from Paul VI on 10 January 1977, with George Basil Cardinal Hume of Westminster as the president. Archbishop Jerzy Stroba of Poznań is secretary. Its headquarters are in St. Gall in neutral Switzerland; meetings are annual. *A Word About [a unified] Europe* was the title of the official declaration of the European Bishops Conference; the declaration was dated 29 June 1977. The Polish pope surely hopes that in due course bishops of the Soviet Baltic Republics will be able to attend.

In John Paul's nomination of eighteen cardinals on 5 January 1983, four were prelates within the Soviet bloc, and one, indeed, Latvian Archbishop Juljans Vaivods of Riga, within the Soviet Union itself. At eighty-seven, Vaivods may have been a sign to the Kremlin that Vatican policy was exclusively spiritual and not politically activist. The pope's ultimate goal may well be not only the nomination of a younger cardinal in Vilnius (already named *in petto*), but also a papal visit to the USSR in 1986 for the sixth centenary of the conversion of the Lithuanians to (Roman) Christianity and possibly another visit in 1988 to Zagorsk, residence of the patriarch of Moscow and counterpart of the monastic *lavra* of Kiev, to celebrate with the patriarch the millennium of the conversion of the sainted Prince Vladimir of Kiev in 988.

Akin perhaps to the involvement of Italianate popes in Italian party politics (primarily with the Christian Democratic party) is Pope Wojtyla's interest in his native Poland. He displays both a residual nationalistic and a wholly cosmopolitan concern. His interest and involvement are all the more direct and delicate

"The New Turn in Church-State Relations in Poland," *Journal of Church and State* 14 (Winter 1982):29-51; see also Hansjakob Stehle, *Eastern Politics of the Vatican, 1917-1979* (Athens: Ohio University Press, 1981).

11. For the text of *Christus Dominus*, see Walter M. Abbott, S.J., ed., *The Documents of Vatican II* (New York: Herder and Herder, Association Press, 1966), pp. 396-429. See esp. §38:4.

because Communist Poland is much more solidly Catholic than the Republic of Italy, which is only somewhat more practicing Catholic than France. It was the experience of national solidarity, joy, hope, and extraordinary self- and group-discipline largely independent of the Polish *Milicja* during the pope's pilgrimage to Poland from 2 to 10 June 1979 that is widely credited with the wholly nonviolent renewal of "Solidarity" in the workers' and peasants' movement under Lech Walesa.[12] In his most political address in Poland, that at Gniezno, John Paul called all Poles "Piasts," sovereigns, which would be like, on his visit to Scotland and Wales, in the presence of the queen of the house of Hanover-Windsor, calling all her subjects "Plantagenets" or "Stuarts."[13]

Apparently, there was an enormous amount of unreported exchange between the late Polish primate Stefan Wyszyński and the pope, including a visit of both the primate and Lech Walesa to Rome; but the first public statement after the pact signed on 31 August 1980 between the party and government and Solidarity, whose elected leader Walesa the pope received and advised and no doubt encouraged to visit Japan and France to gain international visibility, was far from being an espousal of managerial capitalism checked only by trade or industrial unions. Rather, Solidarity represented a theory and policy for work—industrial, agricultural, professional, and cultural—seen as enhancing the dignity of the sovereign person while disposing all citizens to be concerned with the common good, basic to which is "public ownership" (*spoleczny* in the constitution of 1976, not necessarily "state ownership," *państwowy*) of the major enterprises of society under scrupulous national or regional regulations. Distinctive was the recall by Solidarity of socialists and Marxists to the original ideal of factory or industry soviets.[14] Solidarity represented a call and a program for *local* initiative in plants and industries, one in which the managerial role, from

---

12. The impact of the pope's visit to Poland is traced in John P. C. Matthews, "Renewal in Poland," *Worldview* 24 (June 1981):7-10, an essay that could be entitled "How the Pope Helped Bring Poland Together"; see also Gustaw Moszcz, "Walesa: 'Class Defector,'" *The New Statesman* 52 (17 July 1981):11-12. It is an indirect measure of the pope's magnetic effect on his native land that during the first three years of his pontificate there has been a succession of three Communist party secretaries: Edward Gierek, Stanislaw Kania, and, as of 18 October 1981, Wojciech Jaruzelski.
13. For the text of John Paul's address, see *L'Osservatore Romano*, English ed., 11 June 1979, pp. 7-9. The pope delivered the address on 3 June 1979.
14. I.e., factory or industry *rady* (singular, *rada*). The plural form appears in the Polish name for the Union of Soviet Socialist Republics: Zwiazek Socjalistycznych Republik Radzieckich.

foreman up, could be within the power of the workers to advise or to replace. The workers were also encouraged to make procedural suggestions regarding both efficient management and improved production. For all to feel participatory and not indifferent to, or alienated by, daily work was Solidarity's central concern. In holding that the union "shall be independent of all political organizations [i.e., the party] and all organs of state administration,"[15] Solidarity was no doubt accommodating to the facts of life in a Soviet bloc nation. Since party members could enroll in Solidarity and become elected officers, however, it is clear that the fundamental thrust was not anti-Marxist but rather anti-alienationist in the interest of the social, economic, and cultural life of the nation.

One further word of clarification is needed here. The epithet "dissident" is properly attached to one inside the party apparatus who dissents from the policy or even the ideological fine points applied to the unusual situation in Poland, where agriculture has not been extensively collectivized, where commercial and fiscal relations with non-Soviet bloc countries were extensive (and overextended), where the Catholic Church was more powerful in proportion to the population than anywhere else in the entire Second World, and where that same Church had in fact been the bearer of national identity since the final partition of the Polish-Lithuanian Commonwealth in 1795. A proper term describing most non-Communist citizens of Poland who are dissatisfied with the Communist system would be "opponents," members of a theological/ideological (Christian/democratic-socialist) opposition, including most Catholics and others unhappy with any programmatically atheistic government consolidated within boundaries displaced westward after World War II. For tactical reasons, however, the Polish Catholic Church leadership eschew this term, since it can also suggest "disloyal" opposition with a view to the overthrow of the regime and the withdrawal of Poland from the Soviet bloc (with some kind of Western aid); the leadership hence prefer to think of themselves as constructive "critics" within the geopolitical framework. Thus the term "dissenters," which has had a distinguished religio-constitutional history in Poland since 1573,[16] is commonly resorted to

---

15. *Tygodnik Solidarność*, 16 October 1981, p. 1, author's translation.
16. Note the use of this term in the 1573 confessional *Pax dissidentium*. For an English translation and discussion of the confessional, see Earl Morse Wilbur, *A History of Unitarianism: Socinianism and its Antecedents* (Boston: Beacon Press, 1945), pp. 363-64.

for both reform-minded Communists and Christians. To be sure, there are varying groups of Catholics who have sought to accommodate Christian social thought to Marxist analysis and also nonreligious humanists who have readily identified themselves with the hierarchy and often with a local parish for the good of academic freedom and other civil liberties espoused by the Catholic Church and Solidarity. Also, before the imposition of martial law, some party dissidents, seeking to give a human face to the ideology of bureaucratically inefficient, insolent, and, on many levels, unusually corrupt management, established personal contacts with members of the hierarchy and lay faithful concerned with the common good of the system. The "critics/opponents" and surely the "dissidents," as narrowly defined, however, were not, with rare exceptions, seeking to overthrow the party or the government or to detach Poland from the Soviet bloc, although some did hope that their reforming principles would serve as leaven in Soviet societies (hence the eventual charge of "Trotskyism" and of alliance with the CIA). It should be said that many members of the Polish American Congress, which had been organized during World War II to prevent just what happened with the Yalta Agreement, would again dream of more than helping Solidarity *within* the Yaltan boundaries.[17]

The independent, self-governing trade union Solidarity accepted a revised and amended statute and a program of twenty-one postulates at Gdańsk on 16 and 17 August 1980.[18] Postulate three called for all religious confessions to be given equal access to the media and the right of censor-free publication. The pact between Solidarity and the Communist party and government was signed at Gdańsk on 31 August 1980. Recurrent strikes continued pending the expected implementation of the agreement.

A golden age of euphoria and almost reckless hope would for a scant sixteen months draw strength from hidden reserves of national courage and also resentment, in which pre-Yaltan Polish aspirations found here and there understandable expression in such symbols as the recrowned White Eagle and perhaps also in tactical implementation. John Paul published a letter of 28

---

17. Cf., for example, Polish American Conference, *Sprawozdania Prezesa Zarzadu Wykonawczego Poszczególnych Komisji i Kanitetów Wydziałów Stanowych i Biur Kongresu P. A. w Chicago i w Washingtonie na druga Konwenc je Kongresu Polonii Amerykańskiej w Philadelphia, Pa., 29-30-31 maja 1948* (Chicago: Dziennika Zwiazkowego i Zgody, 1948), and subsequent protocols of the congress (e.g., Polish American Conference, *Protokół czwartego Zjazdu Rady Naczelnej Kongresu Polonii Amerykańskiej odbytego w dniach 11-12 października 1954 w hotelu Raleigh, Washington, D.C.* [Washington, 1954]).
18. For the text of this agreement, see *Tygodnik Solidarność*, 16 October 1981, pp. 1-16.

March 1981 to Primate Wyszyński that implied that reports coming to the Holy See from all over Poland were suggesting that a general "will to work and not to strike" had come to prevail, a communication that was intended to strengthen the primate's hand in urging moderation to the headstrong union.[19] The next day, 29 March, in an almost unprecedented act of dealing with the internal affairs of a state, albeit his native land, the pope, in the interest of moderation and of forestalling a Soviet invasion, virtually designated Lech Walesa, in the context of the Helsinki Accords, as the undisputed leader of all factions within Solidarity.[20] The pope reiterated his assertion of the right of Poland as a sovereign power to solve its socioeconomic problems without outside interference. He carefully eschewed reinforcing his warning with political phrases, however. He repeatedly stressed that Vatican City was a signatory of the Helsinki Accords.

After the death of Wyszyński on 28 May 1981 and a *papally* imposed period of a month's mourning (the People's Republic had declared such a period up through the funeral), John Paul appointed Józef Glemp, for two years bishop of Warmia but essentially Wyszyński's closest associate in the primatial curia, as the new primate. After the annual meeting of Solidarity at Gdańsk, which had elected Walesa for a new term (with only 55 percent of the vote) against three more radical candidates, John Paul received Glemp and the president of the Polish Episcopal Conference for at least two hours of deliberation on the policy of the Catholic Church in Poland.

On 13 December 1981 martial law was imposed by General Wojciech Jaruzelski, at once head of the armed forces, the party, and the government and chairman of the Council for the Rescue of the Country (WRON). Jaruzelski had evidently for some time considered the possible arrest of Walesa and many of the leaders of Solidarity, along with some sympathizers among academic and other professional people. In the Diet he initially promised the eventual implementation of the August 1980 agreement, with strictures.

This catastrophe is to be explained in part as follows. The government, the party, and the armed forces were on an unintentioned collision course with Solidarity even while the afore-

---

19. John Paul II to Wyszyński, 28 March 1981, printed in *L'Osservatore Romano*, 29 March 1981, p.1
20. *L'Osservatore Romano*, 29 March 1981, p. 1; *National Catholic Reporter* 17 (1 April 1981):2-3.

mentioned meetings in Gdańsk were in progress. The Gdańsk agreement was to have gone into effect on 1 January 1982. It was the parallelism of the organizations, the party and Solidarity, that caused abrasive interactions, both personal and collective at the local and national levels, that finally melted down the two structures into molten social metal that flowed swiftly and, it seems, inevitably into the ingots of economic, social, and political rigidities characterized by the cold imposition of martial law, an alternative deemed better than Soviet invasion.

The originally eighteen palatinates (voivodeships) of the People's Republic had by 1973 become forty-nine, all with a degree of autonomy and differentiation less than that of the ethnic republics of Yugoslavia but much greater than most of the outside world understood. A voivode was appointed by the central government and the party but had considerable local self-rule through local elections to the palatine presidium from districts, plants and agricultural communes, and other entities entitled to participate in party and administrative affairs. Although most workers were Catholic, few would have been elected to the higher positions; there were only six Catholic deputies in the Diet of Warsaw when martial law was imposed. Solidarity had all along been building its parallel "nonpolitical" units, with their presidia, all the way to the highest presidium with its headquarters in Gdańsk. The dissolution of the Solidarity system within or alongside the discredited system of the United Workers' party (i.e., the Communist party) was perhaps more nearly inevitable than a Soviet invasion or even the mobilization of Soviet units stationed strategically in Poland but seldom visible in the streets or even about their barracks.

By 1 February 1982 the government had declared that 70 percent of all industry was related to national defense and had extended the loyalty oath of 17 December 1981 (for officials) to 70 percent of the workers. On 6 January Primate Glemp had responded to this first major act of the military government—the requirement that every person take a loyalty oath. Glemp said from the pulpit of the cathedral in Warsaw: "Extraction of such declarations is unethical. There is a clear principle also respected by our civil code, that declarations made under duress are not valid."[21] But the primate indirectly advised people to sign the declarations, since they were "meaningless." They were not

---

21. *L'Osservatore Romano*, English ed., 11 January 1982, p. 15; see also *New York Times*, Late ed., 8 January 1982, pp. A1, A8.

meaningless, however, because infraction subjected one no longer to the civil but to the criminal code. Many were disappointed, looking for an issue around which to rally. On Sunday, four days later, the pope assailed the oaths "as abhorrent to the Christian conscience."[22] Perhaps no pope in modern times had ever been so specific about the internal affairs of any other state except Italy, where the pope can speak as any primate. It was clear, moreover, that the primate on the spot and the Polish pope in Rome were temperamentally different; their different roles, however, could be coordinated.

Beginning on 4 February 1982 Glemp and the archbishops of Cracow and Wroclaw (the latter two more resistant to Jaruzelski than Glemp) met with the pope in the Vatican to map a new strategy to salvage the gains of Gdańsk. Afterwards the pope visited French-speaking Gabon, with a majority of its population Catholic, and English-speaking Nigeria, a large, rich, and stable state, two countries where indirectly he might gain some Third World support for Solidarity in the U.N. Commission on Human Rights, which was meeting during February in Geneva, as also concurrently among the signatory powers of the Helsinki Accords, which were meeting on the ministerial level in Madrid.[23] In Lagos on 16 February 1982 the pope said to the Polish community and to the world: "We fight [with Solidarity] for our freedom and for yours."[24] Soon after the return of the three Polish prelates, Glemp, on 27 February and in the name of the Polish episcopate, demanded an end of martial law, the release of the Solidarity internees, and amnesty for prisoners arrested under martial law. These demands surely reflected recent papal instructions.

The entire European political policy of John Paul now stands in grave peril, as does his strongest ecumenical concern, the reunion of the Orthodox and Roman Churches during his pontificate. Such a reunion would include the Patriarchal Church of Moscow and therewith the restoration of freedom to Catholics in the Soviet Union. So direct a challenge was the imposition of martial law by a Polish government on its own people—the pope was surely privy to the exact degree the martial action was an authentic *Polish* military measure—that one can truly say that

22. *L'Osservatore Romano*, English ed., 18 January 1982, p. 3; see also *New York Times*, Late ed., 11 January 1982, p. 9.
23. *L'Osservatore Romano*, 18 February 1982, p. 2.
24. Ibid., author's translation. John Paul has used this line before, but here he was in the presence of the Polish ambassador to Nigeria.

the ethical, international, and ecumenical goals of his entire pontificate are bound up with his success in restoring, to some degree, the *status quo ante* through the Catholic hierarchy and loyal following among the faithful in Poland.

It is surprising in this light that John Paul allowed himself to appear photographed in three different audiences on the Polish issue in the American administration's propaganda film "Let Poland Be Poland."[25] He was filmed with the heads of state or prime ministers of many NATO countries that support President Reagan's sanctions against Jaruzelski and the Kremlin. Although not fully compromised (these were but shots of his own independent actions), the pope could not but have known that the photographs would be treated by the Kremlin and by the Polish Military Council as part of a continuous series of offenses. His failure to prohibit use of the reels was possibly his most serious tactical blunder.

In the meantime in Poland, Primate Glemp, having been authorized at the 183d Plenary of the episcopal conference to revive the Social Council [of specialists] Advisory to the Primate,[26] received the recommendations of the council on 5 April 1982. Aware of the "hatred" and "deep anger" present in all sectors of Polish society, and recognizing that it was the responsibility of the Church to subdue these destructive feelings lest violence overwhelm the nation, the council called for, "in extraordinary times" requiring extraordinary means, a "new social agreement" or "contract" to be arrived at by dialogue among all sectors of society: the government, Solidarity, Rural Solidarity, other unions, professional associations, reorganized student bodies, and the Church as represented primarily by the bishops but also by the clubs of *inteligencja*, which include more than academics. While acknowledging certain political excesses and other failings of Solidarity, as well as the geopolitical and economic realities to be faced by the government, the council demanded as essential the restoration of the Gdańsk agreement of 31 August 1980, the release of arrested leaders and other internees, the government's declaration of immunity to all who had gone into hiding, and its renunciation of an earlier policy of release for all labor leaders who would promise to leave the country. This much was necessary, the council reporting to the primate said, to create the barest foundation for confidence in

---

25.   The title of the film was taken from the hymn "Zeby Polska byla Polska."
26.   This council was first called into being by August Cardinal Primate Hlond, Wyszyński's predecessor.

prospective dialogue. The council called for local nominations and elections that would lead to national councils, separate from the party and the Diet, that in turn would engage in detailed negotiations in which, for their part, workers and their allies would from the start renounce any political goal and limit themselves to points relating to free participation in a healed society. To forestall further despair or violence on the part of the youth, special measures most hated were singled out.[27]

May Day is in Poland, as elsewhere in the Soviet bloc, a holiday; 3 May marks the commemoration of the reformed Polish-Lithuanian Constitution of 1791. Both days were observed by resisters at the cathedral in Warsaw, the first as, in effect, Solidarity Day. In the follow-up on 3 May the chant was heard, "Long live the primate," and this time tear gas and water cannon were used against the fervid demonstrators. Glemp responded with his characteristic condemnation of violence, as though each side were partly to blame. It is clear that he did see variations of opinion within the military government and could understand the problems from the point of view of the government, although he ran the risk of being charged with docility. The pope himself on that same day of the ancient constitution declared: "Since 13 December [1981] I have been suffering again [an allusion to the attack of 13 May 1981] with my nation."[28]

Acting on some ten theses of the council of various specialists, the Polish Episcopal Conference on 14 July 1982 now called for the implementation of the theses so long as three "essentials"[29] were safeguarded in the light of Poland's geopolitical and military status and its economic worsening. The conference then went on to advocate "the lifting of Western sanctions" against Poland, which only "aggravate the crisis," "imperiling Poland's independence."[30]

On 20 July 1982 the Polish foreign minister talked for an

---

27. The recommendation of the Social Council is not directly accessible. It is known to the author from German Bishops Conference, *Bericht* (Report) on the Polish Situation, Summer 1982, Unpublished.
28. *L'Osservatore Romano*, English ed., 18 May 1981, p. 11.
29. The "three essentials" were not spelled out in the *Bericht*. They would presumably be the recognition of Poland as part of the Warsaw Pact, the recognition of the Communist party's "guiding role" in the country (cf. the Polish Constitution of 1976), and the acceptance of a solely economic role for a revived Solidarity not embodied in a political party.
30. German Bishops Conference, *Bericht*. It is clear, in retrospect, that the bishops under Glemp felt, as a whole, that "the common good," a euphemism for the support of a nominally Polish government, should be upheld as better than direct Soviet intervention.

hour with the pope at Castel Gondolfo. It was apparent that the
military government was not prepared to meet the pope's conditions[31] concerning a visit for the observance of the sixth centenary of the arrival of the Black Madonna in Czestochowa; the
government indeed intended to forestall the visit for a year. On
22 July, Poland's National Day, the government made some partial concessions. On 6 August processions to Czestochowa, in
unprecedented numbers, started off from Warsaw and other cities to reach the goal of this national pilgrimage on the Feast of
the Assumption of Mary on 15 August. On 7 August the primate, in a pastoral letter read from all pulpits in Poland,
declared that, despite "the enormous conciliatory efforts of all
social groups," the political authorities "did not express their
approval of the pope's visit"—for the present.[32] On 13 August,
the eight-month commemoration of the "state of war," Solidarity sympathizers demonstrated in Gdańsk, some altering the
national anthem to "March, March, Walesa." On 15 August, at
Czestochowa, referring to agricultural gifts offered to the Virgin
on the Feast of the Assumption and speaking ostensibly of
farmers, Glemp addressed the current scene: "The dialogue
could begin . . . and relieve the hatred [that] can sometimes be
invisible but still exists when people keep silent and grind their
teeth." There is a natural right to organize.[33]

In these straitened circumstances perhaps the pope could see
small advantage in having the young primate gain stature without the papal presence at Czestochowa on 26 August 1982.
Moreover, there are some in the Polish episcopate who hold the
view, possibly shared even by the pope, that Solidarity went too
far not only in the political direction of rivaling the government
but also in the social direction of challenging the role of the
Church as the bearer of national identity, since Solidarity had
moved into charity, education, social criticism, and publication.

The Monday after the canonization of Maksymilian Kolbe of
Auschwitz, the pope, in his *ad limina* of 11 October 1982 to the
Polish bishops, seems to have begun to resign himself to the
demise of Solidarity; he was content to speak of "the fiduciary

---

31. It would appear that Foreign Minister Józef Czyrek was prepared to offer the
government's invitation/permission only on condition that the pope would endorse the
regime as in some way economically and socially necessary in a crisis and would adhere
to the government's limited itinerary for him.
32. Archbishop Józef Glemp, Pastoral Letter, 7 August 1982, Unpublished; see *New
York Times*, Late ed., 6 August 1982, p. A5.
33. *New York Times*, Late ed., 16 August 1982, sec. 1, p. 10; see also p. 1.

role of the Church in defending the legitimate national and civil rights" and Christian culture.[34] Events moved swiftly. Primate Glemp was made privy by the government to tapes and pictures allegedly compromising Walesa, all purportedly made while the labor leader was confined (of which, even if authentic, only Walesa's confessor should have taken note). The strike called by the underground leaders for 10 November 1982, the second anniversary of the registration of Solidarity, coinciding with the death of Brezhnev, was a dismal failure. The next day, the government announced that Walesa, along with several hundred other witnesses, was being released. On 29 November Glemp called for the end of the boycott of the Actors Union against appearance on state-run television; the government abolished the union the next day. On 5 December, a communiqué of the Polish Bishops Conference was read from the pulpits. The communiqué asked the faithful to prepare themselves spiritually for the papal visit to the Black Madonna set to begin on 18 June 1983 for an extended sixth centenary jubilee. On 13 December 1982, Walesa, on a legal pretext, was driven in circles in a government Mercedes-Benz to prevent his planned commemorative address at the monument of slain workers in Gdańsk. At midnight on 30/31 December martial law was formally suspended, but with ample provisions to prevent the embers of Solidarity from flaring up again. On 3 January 1983 the new shop unions were set up to replace the independent union. On 5 January the pope named among the new cardinals Primate Glemp. In a prayer to the Virgin on 12 January, he left it to her whether or not he would actually make the June pilgrimage to her Polish capital. On 30 January Cardinal Glemp confirmed the papal visit for June, urging the youth to cooperate, while also calling on the government "for full amnesty and social justice."

The special concern of the pope for his homeland is closely related to his never clearly enunciated support of a united Europe at peace with itself, conscious of itself as the creative "continent" of old Christendom. Although now seriously secu-

---

34. *L'Osservatore Romano*, 11-12 October 1982, p. 4. Although the pope and the primate seem to have distanced themselves from Solidarity, a pseudonymous Solidarity writer, writing from Poland on 16 November 1982, is unwilling to be unequivocally judgmental (Maciej Poleński, "Miedzy Kleska a Zwyciestwen" ["Between Defeat and Victory"], *Biuletyn Informacyjny* [New York], 13 January 1983, pp. 29-30), while Richard Spielman holds that the leadership of Solidarity exceeded in practice and rhetoric its stated goals (Richard Spielman, "Avoiding a Showdown in Poland," *Foreign Policy* 49 [Winter 1982-83]:20-36).

larized and insofar as religious still divided and ideologically polarized, Europe, according to John Paul, is susceptible to some kind of spiritual and even cultural, quasi-political reunion. Paul VI had declared Saint Benedict of Nursia patron of Europe in 1964. In 1967 he gave canonical status to the Council of European Bishops. In the apostolic letter *Egregiae virtutis*, dated 31 December 1980,[35] John Paul II declared Saints Cyril and Methodius, who had been missionaries among the Slavs under joint sponsorship by Constantinople and Rome, copatrons with Benedict of a Europe spreading from Ireland to the Urals. The pope is quietly working for an economic and cultural confederation of fatherlands. It was with this in mind that John Paul founded for pilgrims to Rome from Poland and the diaspora (Polonia) the Institute of Polish Christian Culture, the director of which is Professor Stanislaw Grygiel of Cracow. At the same time, with the endorsement of the pope, Grygiel launched in 1982 a trimestrial review of culture, *Il Nuovo Areopago*, with an editorial board drawn from both sides of the European ideological divide. Grygiel, in close contact with the pope, envisages the review as embodying the unitive themes of "our European culture." The name of the periodical is taken, of course, from Mars Hill (the Areopagus), where Paul stood to deliver his speech to the Athenians about the unknown God and the resurrection of that God's Son from death.[36] Grygiel, in his rationale for the new periodical, points out that Greek civilization, from which sprang that of Europe, developed between Athens and Sparta, and that even in philosophical Athens the very place of discourse and judgment was the Hill of Mars, which he then juxtaposes with Mount Calvary. Grygiel points out that in the Europe of today, whether "democratic" or "totalitarian," there still prevails the same "iron law of slavery imposed by the materialism of civilization which excludes the liberty of the Resurrection" and which upholds, like the Epicureanism of the Areopagus, "the *wisdom* of death with limits on human possibilities," "the totalary culture of death."[37] In these statements Grygiel reflects the pope's convictions concerning the essential unity of the old "continent" of Christendom, a unity that must be culturally and ecumenically fostered and eventually given political form. In Nigeria, for example, speaking to some three hundred Poles on 16 February

---

35. For the Latin text of this letter, see *Acta Apostolica Sedis* 74 (December 1980):00; for an English translation, see *L'Osservatore Romano*, English ed., 19 January 1981, pp. 3-4.
36. Acts 17:16-32.
37. Grygiel's Announcement of *Il Nuovo Areopago*, Unpublished.

1982, the pope, with the developments in Poland very much on his mind, nevertheless still thought as a cosmopolitan Pole of the latent unity of the continent whence he and they came. He spoke as no Italian pope would have to Italians abroad of "our Fatherland and its neighbors, of *our* continent" in contrast to Africa or Asia.[38]

It is evident from a close reading of all the pope's messages over a two-year period about Benedict, on the occasion of the patron's fifteenth centenary and in connection with the pope's earlier visit to the scene of the Polish battle of Monte Cassino on his own fifty-ninth birthday, that John Paul II has woven a rather tight tapestry of religio-political policy with respect to Europe, despite the fact that Christianity in many parts of NATO and the Iron Curtain countries is either in retreat or under oppression.[39] He looks for the possible military neutralization of several central European countries, an act that would allow the reunification of the two Germanies and the withdrawal of Soviet and NATO forces to the margins of the two blocs; he resists the placement of neutron bombs anywhere in Europe.

John Paul made specific his thoughts about Germany at the reception at Castle Augustusburg in Brühl near Bonn in the presence of Federal President Karl Carstens and Chancellor Helmut Schmidt on 15 November 1980. After paying tribute to the diligence and resourcefulness of the citizens in rebuilding their part of Germania and in sharing most generously their wealth with developing nations, the pope said: "There has still remained for your people, however, the painful division which—as I hope—may find its fitting peaceful solution in a united Europe."[40] By a united Europe it is clear from several statements that the pope has in mind more than Latin Christendom. He includes Yugoslavia (with two of its federated states Catholic) and even Greece. A united Europe would mean, in effect, at least a third force between the Soviet Union and North America—economic, cultural, spiritual, and necessarily military. The pope seems to hope, through union with the Patriarchal Church of Moscow, the Ecumenical Patriarchate in Istanbul, and the Auto-

38. *L'Osservatore Romano*, 18 February 1982, p. 2, author's translation.

39. A number of the pope's utterances concerning a united Europe may be found in George Huntston Williams, "*Dialogi* of Today's Gregory the Great," Address at St. John's University, Collegeville, Minn., 6 April 1981. The subject of this address was Saint Benedict as patron saint of Europe.

40. *L'Osservatore Romano*, 17-18 November 1980, p. 3, author's translation. A complete English translation of the pope's remarks appears in *L'Osservatore Romano*, English ed., 1 December 1980. See also Williams, "*Dialogi* of Today's Gregory the Great," §3.

cephalous Church of the Republic of Cyprus, to be involved in a spiritual pan-European union.

In turning now to John Paul's relations with traditionally non-Christian states, attention must be given to the complex relationship of the Holy See sovereign in Vatican City to the Jewish State of Israel, which is only partly analogous in nature to the Vatican. That Jerusalem is the capital of a restored Eretz Israel penetrates the marrow and lifts the heart of almost every member of the world Jewish community and indeed gives meaning to the Holocaust and all antecedent sufferings in Jewish faithfulness to the covenant. Because of the holocaust of six million Jews, most of these in camps in the pope's homeland, world Jewry deplores the fact that John Paul seems to have no more empathy for their misshapen homeland state than previous popes. Israel is not internationally recognized as in rightful possession of what once constituted the main part of historic Israel. Surrounded by Arab states, Israel is nevertheless something like what Vatican City is for Catholics in giving Jews all over the world geographical, cultural, spiritual, and almost soteriological security. In a remarkable way, the establishment of their state has also revived their ancient language, Hebrew, the counterpart of the Latin of vestigial Rome that survives in the studies, chambers, chapels, and corridors of Saint Peter's sacred precincts and in its most solemn documents. Of course Israel, however, is a state not only with ambassadors, scholars, bankers, businessmen, and technicians all over the world, but also, unlike Vatican City, with a puissant military establishment and the capability to manufacture and export munitions.

Even if within Israel all religions are free to exercise almost plenary rights under the constitution, an ability not thinkable within the limited precincts of Vatican City, the fact remains that Israel with Jerusalem, sacred to the devotees of three religions, is a Jewish state, even if "Jewish" is construed more in an ethnic or communitarian than in a confessional sense. In any case, the policy of John Paul toward Israel has not yet been fully articulated; his acts and utterances, however, revelatory of one aspect of his church-state thought and policy, suggest that he might be more conservative than his four predecessors. In line with them he does not recognize the State of Israel, this fact in appeal to the time-hallowed precedent of not recognizing any state until a peace treaty has confirmed its status and boundaries among the nations, although the Vatican did make a choice with respect to the two Germanies, Poland, and Taiwan in the absence of formal peace treaties.

Despite the acknowledgment by Vatican II that old Israel was an elect community and in a sense also an *ecclesia*,[41] precisely its reemergence as a quasi-religious Israeli state among the nations constitutes for the pope a *theological* problem exacerbated by sensibilities and considerations of strategy with regard to Christians living under several Muslim governments, all but one of which is hostile to Israel. This problem is also particularly difficult for John Paul, perhaps, because of his special devotion to the sacred places of Jerusalem.[42] In any case, in 1980, in a six-point position paper for Jimmy Carter (not immediately released at the time of the presidential visit), in speeches before Italian biblical scholars at Castel Gondolfo, and at a commemoration of the Turkish massacre of Catholics in Otranto five centuries earlier, he called for "a united Jerusalem under U.N. guarantees" and went out of his way to deplore the "exclusion" of Palestinians by the creation of the State of Israel.[43] He was more specific in speaking to Israeli Foreign Minister Yitzhak Shamir on 7 January 1981: "[A]n effective contribution will have been made when the Palestinians of the West Bank and the Gaza Strip see that they may enjoy a serene condition in full respect of all their rights."[44]

No change of position was registered toward the State of Israel in the communiqué following Shamir's visit, the first high-level Israeli visit in four years.[45] In June 1982 the pope was vigorous in his condemnation of what could well have reminded him of the *Blitzkrieg* loosed upon his own land on 1 September 1939. Israeli forces, on the pretext of the attempt upon the life of the Israeli ambassador in London by a splinter group of the Palestine Liberation Organization, moved through the populous ancient Lebanese capitals of Sidon and Tyre and terrorized Beirut with bombing from land, sea, and air to rout the Palestinians and Syrians in West Beirut. There were uncounted but enormous civilian casualties. Almost half the Lebanese are Christians, as are many of the Palestinians. Of the Christian Lebanese

---

41. Cf. Williams, "John Paul II's Concepts of Church, State, and Society," at fn. 13. For the pope's use of the term "new Israel," see section four of his homily delivered at Davao, the Philippines, 20 February 1981, printed in *L'Osservatore Romano*, 21 February 1981, p. 3, and in John Paul II, *The Pope to the Filipino People*, p. 102.
42. Williams, *The Mind of John Paul II*, pp. 170-71. Cf. the pope's attachment to Kalwaria Zebrzydowska (Williams, *The Mind of John Paul II*, pp. 38, 40-41, 74-76, 280).
43. Ibid., p. 328.
44. *L'Osservatore Romano*, 8 January 1982, p. 1, author's translation.
45. See ibid.

almost two-thirds are Uniate Catholic of four rites: Maronite, Melchite, Armenian Catholic, and Chaldean. Israel had as its initial ally in the invasion Commander Major Saad Haddad, a Maronite, who had already created on 15 April 1979 a "Free Lebanon" (the Haddad Militia Zone, south of the U.N. Zone), in which more than half of the inhabitants are Shi'ite Muslims. A former officer of the central Lebanese Army, Haddad had roughly the same goals as Israel: to drive out the PLO and the Syrians. Despite this Christian ally and the prospects of an independent, internally strong Lebanon, one reconstructed after intra-Lebanese warfare and the Israeli-Haddad invasion, Israel has irreparably lost good will by its action with the *Sovrano* of Vatican City. It was left vague as to whether Mother Teresa, who called on the pope before her departure and landed at Beirut under Israeli bombardment of civilians on 13 August 1982, was designated by John Paul as "a personal emissary."[46] If so, the gesture involving two Nobel laureates of peace, symbolically at either end of the firing tanks, was dramatic. Mother Teresa, however, had no direct words for Menachem Begin or his minister of defense but said only that she came to visit the hospital of her order, the Sisters of Charity, and would do what she could to relieve suffering. (When "Christians" later massacred Palestinians in two camps in Beirut, the pope deplored the horrendous event but had no special rebuke for them as Catholics under his jurisdiction as well as under Israeli direction.)

With respect to John Paul's relations with other primarily non-Christian states, the papal visit to secularized Muslim Turkey (where at the capital, Ankara, the pope was unable to deliver all his prepared communications because of the tight political situation), his visit to Muslim Pakistan en route to the Philippines, and that to the Muslim head of state in Lagos and to Muslim leaders elsewhere in Nigeria all indicate that he has still more to say to the political and religious leaders of the Muslim world. Noted already in his visit to the Philippines was his most fully developed address to Muslim citizens of the republic on Mindanao.[47]

Instructive was his visit to Japan from 23 to 26 February 1981. Christianity of all groupings is most minuscule there. Shinto and Buddhism vie and intermingle. Soon after his arrival John Paul took occasion to commend the Emperor Meiji for having granted

---

46. *New York Times*, Late ed., 12 August 1982, p. A16.
47. Williams, "John Paul II's Concepts of Church, State, and Society," at fn. 73.

full religious freedom in Japan in 1889. John Paul caused some controversy, however, when as sovereign he insisted on the protocol of a visit to the Emperor Hirohito. Some Catholic leaders and many Protestants voiced protest at the announced encounter as giving indirect support to the new movement, against the constitutional provision, for the renationalization of Shinto and even the eventual revival of the emperor cult itself. Many older Christians had suffered during World War II for refusing to heed the emperor as divine. Eventually, in protest on the ground that it gave visibility to the process of redeification of the emperor, ten of the thirty-five Protestant and Orthodox representatives invited to the nunciature to meet the pope absented themselves, including the moderator of the National Council of Churches of Japan, Kishimoto Yoichi, who had earlier written of pan-Protestant concern to Asajiro Cardinal Satowaki of Nagasaki on 23 January 1981: "The meeting of the Emperor and the Pope, who is both the supreme religious and political ruler of the Vatican City State, might mislead people into the belief that the Emperor's role as head of the State supersedes the sovereignty of the people."[48]

Many ardent Shintoists for their part protested the encounter for the opposite reason: the undesired contrast between a frail, desacralized symbol and a charismatic, authentic, religious sovereign, the Vicar of Christ. Buddhist leaders were keenly disappointed that the pope would not reciprocate their visitations to him in Vatican City by visiting one of their principal shrines; the leaders were instead bidden to meet with him in the apostolic nunciature in Tokyo.

In receiving seven bishops from Zimbabwe on 18 June 1982, a country that is 96 percent black and only about 20 percent Christian of all denominations, the pope urged them, on the occasion of their first *ad limina* visit to Rome (every five years), not to lose their ecclesial identity by supporting only one political party. This asseveration is all the more important because the chief of state is a Catholic: "No political group can arrogate to itself the right to represent her [the Church]"; "the teaching of Christ . . . can never be confused with that of any political party." He urged collaboration, after ten years of civil war of several factions, with persons of all tribes and of both races for

---

48.   Yoichi to Satowaki, 23 January 1981, quoted in *Japan Christian Activity News*, 20 February 1981, p. 5. Cf. Peter Hebblethwaite, "Timing of Pope's Japan Visit Creates . . . Touchy Relations," *National Catholic Reporter* 17 (6 March 1981):20-21.

the common good and for the removal of "many obstacles . . . for the accomplishment of the work of evangelization."[49]

With respect to provisional governments, organizations, and armies, terrorist or conventional, John Paul has spoken in general terms in the encyclical *Dives in misericordia*.[50] He sought in this work to reassure men and women of good will that the extermination camps of his environing youth, the terror of the nihilistic Red Brigade in Italy and its counterparts in Federal Germany and elsewhere, all forms of piracy, highjacking, kidnapping, and systematic terror and political torture, are aberrations in the design of the God of mercy and that people of good will may take heart that goodness will still prevail and violence surely fail.

As to specific acts, somewhat puzzling was the papal mission of Archbishop Hilarion Ciappi, once of Jerusalem and an ardent defender of the PLO, to the American hostages in Iran.[51] Much more in keeping with the pope's loathing of violence was his dispatch of Father John Maggee to Ulster in April 1981. This Ulster-born priest, who guided the pope's pilgrimage to Ireland in September 1979, asked all to renounce violence in the name of His Holiness, including suicidal fasting in Maze Prison in Belfast, and thereafter visited the recently bereaved families on either side of the partly confessional struggle.[52] The strategy of fasting to death was abandoned by the Provisional Irish Republican Army on 2 October 1981. The pope may have had privy knowledge that, although the splinter group of the IRA had the sympathy of many ordinary Catholics (but not of the priests or of any bishops), it was in league with larger revolutionary and terroristic forces in Europe at large and that it had intentions to subvert in its radical direction even the Republic of Ireland.

On 15 September 1982, to the surprise of most, the pope received in private audience Chairman Yasser Arafat of the PLO. On 6 March 1983 in El Salvador the pope, deploring violence on both sides, denounced violent social change and called for dialogue, meaning, in the circumstances, negotiations between the government and the insurgents.

---

49.   *L'Osservatore Romano*, 19 June 1981, p. 1, author's translations.
50.   For the text of *Dives in misericordia*, see *L'Osservatore Romano*, English ed., 9 December 1980, pp. 9-18. The encyclical was promulgated on 30 November 1980.
51.   Williams, *The Mind of John Paul II*, p. 324.
52.   *L'Osservatore Romano*, 30 April 1981, p. 1; *L'Osservatore Romano*, 2-3 May 1981, pp. 1-2.

SUPRANATIONAL POLITICAL ENTITIES AND THE QUASI-POLITICAL
ENTITIES OF EVERY SOCIETY: THE EXPANSION OF SUBSIDIARITY[53]

The Syntax of Global Communication. On the global scene, John
Paul goes further and with greater specificity than his great
predecessors John XXIII and Paul VI in his exertions for peace
and global economic justice. In his message on world peace for 1
January 1980 he made good use of his skills as philologist and
actor to call upon the diplomats and other spokesmen of the
nations to use care in speech, to make concessions in rhetoric in
order to imagine the reality of the situation as perceived by the
potential adversary, and thus to prepare the verbal ground for
realistic negotiation without posturing.[54] He called upon diplomats and international lawyers to freshen the meaning of words
in communication among themselves—to eschew exaggeration,
to state the essentials, all in order that each side might get in
focus the true needs of the other and prepare for concessions
without these being considered signs of weakness on either side.
John Paul believes in the saving power of the honest and careful
word in international relations. His own style of speech before
the U.N. in New York, and before UNESCO in Paris and
Hiroshima in June 1980 and February 1981, respectively, illus-
trate the new papal vocabulary and syntax. He speaks to the
nations as a man of reason to reasonable spokesmen of the
peoples.

Interhemispheric Economic and Social Justice. In many addresses,
notably in his U.N. address and speech in Yankee Stadium during his October 1979 visit to the United States, and almost
always at least once in an appropriate place in every developed
country, John Paul has called for the redistribution of the wealth
of the world between the northern and the southern hemi-
spheres, not merely of the surplus ("crumbs").[55] Growing out of
his prepapal conception of the "global neighbor" and hence of
the ecumenical church of humanity, John Paul holds aloft the

---

53. See Williams, "John Paul II's Concepts of Church, State, and Society," at fn. 39.
As noted in this earlier essay, Pius XI, in *Quadragesimo anno*, defined "subsidiarity" as "a
fundamental principle of social philosophy, fixed and unchangeable, that one should not
withdraw from individuals and commit to the community what they can accomplish by
their own enterprise and industry."
54. Williams, *The Mind of John Paul II*, p. 323.
55. John Paul has spoken on this topic frequently, in Italy, in France at UNESCO in
June 1980, in Federal Germany in November 1980, in Japan in February 1981, and in
Switzerland at the June 1982 meeting of the World Labor Organization at Geneva.

Good Samaritan as the world ideal for persons and nations,[56] most poignantly and vividly in his appeal of 21 February 1981 from an East Asian refugee camp in Bataan in the Philippines, wherein the Good Samaritan was the "symbol of solidarity" with all the refugees of the world.[57]

Himself the son of a soldier, John Paul has fully interiorized the martial motif in calling for inner discipline also in intranational social and political change. He appeals to the conscience of those in power, economically and politically, to make maximal, not minimal, concessions for the common good, not gradually but swiftly, lest the powerful be faced with the expropriation of their property, an alternative that he approves as a last resort.[58] In his two pilgrimages to Africa, John Paul found occasion to speak forcefully against the replication of colonial exploitation by the new indigenous elites and bureaucrats with tribal loyalties and against the native economic-military complex that upholds several postcolonial native administrations, which often are corrupt and self-serving. At the same time, the pope urged the downtrodden and disadvantaged not to resort to violence or to be lured by "alien ideologies" that will eventually impoverish them spiritually and will not necessarily be economically advantageous. In countries where unionization of labor is against the law or restricted to company unions, however, John Paul has legitimated strikes—in Brazil, in Poland, in the Philippines. He has called for the legitimization of documentless or migrant workers in order that they may be less easily exploited (the United States, France, West Germany), a theme also prominent in *Laborem exercens*.[59]

In Brazil the pope gave qualified support to "base communities" sponsored by several progressive cardinals and bishops.[60] He chose, however, not to visit such a quasi-political compound.[61] In the Philippines John Paul became precise: the

---

56. See Karol Wojtyla, *The Acting Person*, ed. Anna-Teresa Tymieniecka, trans. Andrzej Potocki, Analecta Husserliana, vol. 10 (Dordrecht, The Netherlands: D. Reidel Publishing Co., 1979), pp. 261-99. For a discussion on the text of *The Acting Person*, see Williams, "John Paul II's Concepts of Church, State, and Society," fn. 18.

57. *L'Osservatore Romano*, English ed., 2 March 1981, p. 12.

58. The pope has expressed this position several times, particularly in speeches given in Mexico, Brazil, and the Philippines.

59. *Laborem exercens*, §23. For the Latin text of *Laborem exercens*, see *Acta Apostolicae Sedis* 73 (5 November 1981):577-647; for an English translation, see *Tablet* (London) 235 (26 September 1981):235-42, (3 October 1981):964-69. See also Williams, "John Paul II's Concepts of Church, State, and Society," at fn. 36.

60. The German theorist of this political theology of the poor is Johann Metz.

61. Cf. Williams, "John Paul II's, Concepts of Church, State, and Society," §4.

Church, both priests and laymen, must support the poor "not to demand charity, but to ask for justice" so that work will never degrade.[62] He continued to think less in terms of a church *of* the people, however, and more in the "paternalistic" or the "bourgeois" church *for* the people.[63] He seemed to carry over from his experience and formation in the Second World (which is founded upon the Marxist revolutions of 1917 and 1945) so intense a concern for the rights of the "human person" as these rights were once achieved by the "bourgeois" or middle class in several long-since receding revolutions (1647/88, 1776, 1789, 1848) that he may still be unprepared to recognize the troubled emergence of an authentic postbourgeois, radical communitarian personal freedom of the type now crying for Catholic-socialist expression in the Third World, particularly in Latin America and to some small extent in the Philippines and in some formerly French Southeast Asian countries. This inability holds despite his explicit interest in dialogue and his orientation to the Third World in concern for its poverty and the powerlessness of its (Catholic) masses.[64]

The Specifics of World Peace. John Paul, who as a youth chose first the conspiratorial theater and then the seminary rather than the resistance movement (unlike so many of his generation), stood on 18 May 1979 at the cemetery of a thousand Poles who had died on the slopes of Monte Cassino. He visited the cemetery in order to commemorate the thirty-fifth anniversary of a renowned Polish victory in World War II, a day by coincidence his own fifty-ninth birthday. Surrounded by survivors of the men who fought under General Wladyslaw Anders—Poles of approximately his own age—and the survivors of other national units whose slain were being commemorated at other cemeteries, the *Pontifex Maximus*, applying one of the Ten Commandments to killing *in war*, declared: "Thou shalt not kill!"[65]

To be sure, the pontiff knows all too well that there will be preparations for defense and even many lesser wars. His eyes, however, are on nuclear holocaust, and his heart is turned to the

---

62. *L'Osservatore Romano*, 21 February 1981, p. 2.
63. This distinction is taken from Metz's writings.
64. Cf. the three churches in the typology of Johann Metz: *Volkskirche, Bürgerkirche,* and *Basiskirche* (Johann Baptist Metz, *The Emergent Church: The Future of Christianity in a Postbourgeois World*, trans. Peter Mann [New York: Crossroad Publishing Co., 1981]).
65. *L'Osservatore Romano*, 19 May 1979, p. 8; *L'Osservatore Romano*, English ed., 28 May 1979, pp. 6-7. That this application of the commandment was solemnly intended, see other statements from the commemoration and those given in Williams, "*Dialogi* of Today's Gregory the Great."

causes of violence within the hearts of men and women, even those of kindred blood. Insofar as there are armed forces, he wishes chaplains to be among the military "to bear witness to the Church as expert pastors" yet not involved in any implicable way in the violence of warfare.[66]

John Paul II spoke more than once at Hiroshima. In his address before the U.N. University in Hiroshima on 25 February 1981, "Humanity Must Make a Moral About-Face," he noted with anguish that "about a half of the world's research workers are at present employed for military purposes," that "one soldier's equipment costs many times more than a child's education." In Hiroshima he went further than at the U.N. in October 1979 in denouncing war: "Let us . . . work untiringly for disarmament and the banishing of all nuclear weapons; let us replace violence with confidence and caring . . . . Let humanity never become the victim of a struggle between competing systems; let there never be another war."[67] John Paul has been against tactical nuclear arms among NATO forces, indeed against the further manufacture and any use of atomic weapons.[68] In Washington, D.C., in October 1979, he had supported SALT II.

On 7 and 8 October 1981, in the headquarters of the nondenominational Pontifical Academy of Sciences in Casina Pius IV at Vatican City, President Carlos Chagras with members and testifiers dealt with the threat of nuclear war. Dean Howard Hiatt of Harvard University's School of Public Health, who had spearheaded Physicians Against the Last Epidemic, was a testifier; Professor Victor Weisskopf of the Massachusetts Institute of Technology is a regular member. The report of the academy meeting, on being received by His Holiness, led John Paul to send papal delegations, made up of members and testifiers, to meet with the heads of the five nuclear powers on 14 and 15 December 1981 and with the president of the U.N. Assembly. The Washington and U.N. delegation was led by Weisskopf.

---

66. John Paul II, "Address to the First World Meeting of Chaplains General under the Presidency of Sebastian Cardinal Baggio, Prefect of the Sacred Congregation for Bishops, 1 October 1980," *L'Osservatore Romano*, 10 October 1980, p. 3, author's translation. See also *L'Osservatore Romano*, English ed., 17 November 1980, p. 7. In the concordats (*conventiones*) worked out under John Paul II there is always the provision that the pope name the ranking Catholic chaplain in the armed services of the country.

67. *Japan Times*, 26 February 1981, p. 1; *L'Osservatore Romano*, 26 February 1981, p. 1, author's translation.

68. Cf. his passionate statements in speeches delivered in Paris (before UNESCO), Hiroshima, and Nagasaki.

The pope's purpose was to testify to the awesomeness of nuclear conflict and the consequences for even populations not directly involved and to dramatize the papal moral concern by making use of non-Catholics as well as Catholics. Although President Reagan listened to the papal delegation only briefly, all standing, President Leonid Brezhnev gave the counterpart group a much longer hearing on 15 December; in his communiqué Brezhnev said appreciatively that it was the first papal legation ever received at the Kremlin.[69] The work of the Pontifical Academy continued in a special meeting convened in Vienna in February 1982.

During his pilgrimage to the United Kingdom, then at war with Argentina, the pope spoke frequently against war, having in mind, of course, the conflict in the South Pacific on which both in Britain and later in Argentina he remained strictly neutral. In Britain, however, his statements were of more fundamental character. At Coventry, on 30 May 1982, making allusion to the cathedral reconstructed in reconciliation by many youths from Germany and other countries, he said: "Today, the scale and the horror of modern warfare—whether nuclear or not—make it totally unacceptable as a means of settling differences between nations."[70] To a youth rally in Ninian Park at Cardiff on 2 June 1982, stressing prayer, he said, "When you are in contact with the Prince of Peace, you understand how totally opposed to his message are . . . hatred and war."[71] At the Cardiff airport, taking leave, he held a news conference, and to a German reporter asking about the applicability of Thomas Aquinas's theory of the just war,[72] the pope answered: "It cannot be denied, the right of self-defense; but it is necessary to look for other solutions. Today it is necessary to exclude any war."[73] He

---

69.   Brezhnev, not well versed in Catholic Church history, may be excused for not knowing that, in mutual concern over the Turkish threat, Ivan IV the Terrible received a papal legation under Antonio Possevino in 1582.

70.   *L'Osservatore Romano*, English ed., 7 June 1982, pp. 3-4.

71.   Ibid., pp. 19-20.

72.   Cf. various statements of Terence Cardinal Cooke concerning the just nuclear war over against those of several American episcopal activists who supported a nuclear freeze. The fact that the pope named Joseph Bernardin as cardinal on 5 January 1983 was interpreted by the archbishop of Chicago himself as papal approbation of Bernardin's presiding in Washington over the American Bishops Conference concerning the pastoral letter that urged a nuclear freeze.

73.   *L'Osservatore Romano*, 3 June 1982, p. 2, author's translation. All the papal communications in Britain appear in Peter Jennings, ed., *The Pope in Britain* (London: Bodley Head, 1982); the interview on the plane, however, is reported only in news releases. The pope, in his annual address to the diplomatic corps, said on 15 January 1983 that the Holy See in its "humanitarian concern" was prompted to recommend "clemency and

quoted the above statements" in his address to President Ronald Reagan at Vatican City on 7 June 1982 and prefaced them thus: "[M]any factors in society . . . positively contribute to peace: . . . an increasing realization of the interdependence of all peoples, a growing solidarity with those in need, and a greater conviction of the absurdity of war as a means of resolving controversies."[74]

At the U.N. Assembly's special session on disarmament, the pope, whose address was read by Cardinal Casaroli on 11 June 1982, declared: "Of course, no power, no statesman will admit that he intends to project a war or take the initiative in one. Nevertheless, mutual distrust makes men believe or fear that others nourish such designs, . . . with the result that each seems to envisage no other solution but . . . to get ready a defense force sufficient to reply to eventual attack. . . . If efforts at arms reduction, then total disarmament, are not accompanied and paralleled by ethical renewal, they are already destined to fail."[75]

John Paul places all warfare on the same level as terrorism, torture, inquisition (having deplored its use by the Church itself in the past), brainwashing, violence in the streets, and insurrection. He believes that physical, intellectual, or spiritual violence can only defeat the cause it professes to serve. The Polish pope from the environs of Auschwitz, from a land twice partitioned into nonexistence as a state (1795 and 1939), the philosopher pope of the jet age and of potential nuclear holocaust, speaks at times almost like a pre-Constantinian Christian under recurrent persecution or like an evangelical Anabaptist on the morrow of the Peasants War that raged in sixteenth-century Germany and beyond; like a Christian humanist during the confessional wars that devastated France in the sixteenth century; like a Lutheran Pietist or a Quaker after the partly confessional and schismatic thirty years of war that destroyed more than half the population of Central Europe in the seventeenth century and after the ethnic-confessional civil war that mangled Great Britain and Poland in the same century; like a Herrnhutter in the eighteenth century during endless dynastic wars;[76] and quite unlike

mercy for those condemned to death" (*L'Osservatore Romano*, 17-18 January 1983, p. 2, author's translation).

74. *L'Osservatore Romano*, English ed., 14 June 1982, p. 5.

75. *L'Osservatore Romano*, English ed., 21 June 1982, pp. 3-5. The pope was then in Buenos Aires; see *New York Times*, Late ed., 12 June 1982, p. A4.

76. Concerning the eighteenth century, one thinks of, besides the writings of the Herrnhuter Count von Zinzendorf (d. 1760), Charles Irenée Castel, l'abbé de Saint-Pierre, *Projet de la paix perpetuelle* (1713) and Immanual Kant, *Zum ewigen Frieden* (1795). Both of these works have been translated a number of times. For Saint-Pierre's work, see

his papal predecessor Pius VII (1800-1823), who, while all of Europe was convulsed by Napoleon Bonaparte, thought primarily of episcopacies, concordats, and the Papal States temporarily annexed to the French Empire. There is no pope and perhaps no moral theologian who has plumbed as deeply into the mechanisms and disguises of violence as has John Paul II. He is the first almost pacifist pope in the sense of his having a theory of conduct to countervail the diverse realms of violence. In London and Liverpool he stretched out his hand in blessing on the Reverend Ian Paisely, who in pallor subsided, knowing that somehow the shout of "Antichrist" was not only unseemly but invalidated by the personality of John Paul, however much the Free Presbyterian of Ulster, with his honorary D.D. degree from Bob Jones University, remained fixed in his stand against "popery."

In Defense of All Civil Liberties: The Triumphalist Temptation. Precisely because he harks back to the gospel in his understanding of the cunning of Satan's temptations, as an exponent of the gospel John Paul at once proclaims the liberty of conscience to captives and yet, as vicar of that first proclaimer, finds himself sometimes tempted to symbolize Christ's triumph on Palm Sunday or at the Ascension. John Paul is committed to the principle of the freedom of religion and hence to the separation of church and state as promulgated by the decree of religious liberty of Vatican II, *Dignitas humanae.*[77] Having commented on the decree in his *Sources of Renewal,*[78] he does not intend to take advantage of even vestigial preferential constitutional arrangements and traditions in some states (except for the upholding of concordats guaranteeing the freedom of the Church) to promote the interests of the Catholic Church in relation to other Christians or to devotees of other religions, so long as the freedom of religion in general, private and corporate, is upheld or secured. Indeed, John Paul is the most unequivocal defender of all civil liberties of any pope.[79]

A Project for Perpetual Peace, trans. Edith M. Nuttal (London: R. Cobden-Sanderson, 1927); for Kant's, see *Perpetual Peace*, trans. Nicholas Murray Butler (New York: Columbia University Press, 1939).

77. For the text of *Dignitas humanae*, see Abbott, *The Documents of Vatican II*, pp. 675-96. See esp. §15.

78. See Karol Wojtyla, *Sources of Renewal: The Implementation of the Second Vatican Council*, trans. P. S. Falla (San Francisco: Harper and Row, 1980), pp. 290-93, 408-16. The Polish original is entitled *U podstaw odnowy: Studium o realizacji Vaticanum II* (Cracow: Polskie Towarzystwo Teologiczne, 1972).

79. Williams, *The Mind of John Paul II*, pp. 170-79.

John Paul is putting his particular stamp on the implementation of *Dignitas humanae*. This decree had been shaped in some considerable measure out of the American experience and constitutional context by John Courtney Murray, S.J. (1904-67) and converted from a Catholic "hypothesis" into the Vatican II "thesis" and program. The new thesis was defended personally in the basilica by two interventions of Karol Wojtyla himself, although he was in these speeches careful to explain that the principle stemmed not from "liberal toleration" or "religious indifferentism" but rather from a positive traditional Catholic respect for the inviolability of conscience in the realm of religion.[80] One may regret in these earlier interpretations the Polish prelate's lack of magnanimity in recognizing that it was, in fact, often the sectarians and Protestants who had historically most often pressed and indeed suffered for this "Catholic respect for conscience."[81] Murray had spoken in terms of rights and responsibilities and had come up with a great formula that every Christian American is *civis idem et christianus* ("Both citizen and Christian"). Using a medieval French legist, he sought to derive his theory, now authoritative in the Church, from John of Jandun (d. 1328). Murray did so by the process of seeing the *potestas regalis* devolving in a democracy eventually upon every individual citizen, male and at length female.[82] In all prepapal writings touching upon society and the state, Wojtyla, in a different context, also stressed the individual, the "human person," and his right and responsibility to participate in the communal life, civic and ecclesiastical. Wojtyla is no different in his papal writings. Guided by the principle of subsidiarity,[83] he thinks of the Church in several meanings of the term and of the various units of society, from the family to the state and the temporal infrastructures and suprastructures, as comprised of persons in varying degrees of participation and alienation or indifference and egotism.

John Paul has quietly moved to depoliticize the lower reaches of his far-flung empire of the Spirit, the *sacerdotium*. He activated the canon in the *Codex Iuris Canonici* of 1917 opposed to

---

80. Ibid., pp. 176-79.
81. Ibid., p. 177. For one well versed in Polish history, it is clear that in this case the Catholic majority had indeed acquiesced in favor of religious toleration out of Christian conviction and had eschewed the use of force.
82. For the author's appreciative analysis of Murray's writings up to 1954, see George Huntston Williams, "Issues between Catholics and Protestants at Midcentury," *Religion in Life* 23 (Spring 1954):163-86.
83. See above, fn. 52.

diocesan and religious priests in public office, whether appointive or elective, except by permission of their ordinary or superior. The most conspicuous implementation of this canon was the limitation imposed upon Congressman Robert F. Drinan, S.J., of Massachusetts. A few priests still serve in parliaments and even high in some governments, as in Sandanista Nicaragua. The pope encourages priests and nuns to vote whenever possible, and he has said clearly that the priests and bishops may speak out on social issues and in defense of religious and other civil liberties. Archbishop Raymond Hunthausen of Seattle, Archbishop John Quinn of San Francisco, and other American bishops have doubtless been encouraged by the pope, through teaching and example, in their truly prophetic stand against nuclear arms. John Paul, however, is firmly against the direct involvement of priests in liberation movements and radical theology, even when politicized priests are the only spokesmen of peons against proprietors; he is even more restrictive with respect to the role of nuns and sisters in such movements. The New Code of Canon Law, promulgated on 25 January 1983, reflects his restrictive view.

John Paul himself understands the distinction between critical prophecy and traditional teaching but seems to reserve to himself the distinctively critical function from his sovereign base. He still fully acknowledges episcopal collegiality in the ordinary magisterium of articulating already received truths in faith and morals in application to given local circumstances. It is possible that one is witnessing in the Polish papacy a programmatic monopolization in the Holy See/Vatican City of the politically and socially prophetic role in the Old Testament sense.

One reason for this depoliticizing of priests and nuns is to make possible a globally coordinated show of moral and spiritual force to stave off revolution in the Third World and to bestir Catholic rulers, great landowners, tribal chieftains, and integralist prelates to make social and political changes before time runs out. The pope, with his strong eschatological sense, is deeply concerned to discipline the people of God through the episcopate and the religious orders to the end that they are not conformed to the world but serve as a leaven within the lump of humanity and a light to nations and societies amid great and complex turmoil. Through his own unique position as a tactically neutral *Sovrano* and yet as a teacher of all and an exemplar to many of the gospel ideal, and through his nonconfessional addresses and appeals and the missions of his diplomatic corps he seeks peace, social justice, racial justice, and interhemispheric economic justice.

It must be said, however, that John Paul does not regard all alleged rights as necessarily civil liberties; he is not accessible to the argument (leveled against him by letters from a leading Pentecostal in Brazil and personally by a leading Reformed theologian in France)[84] that his trips, which place heavy burdens on national governments and municipalities for his protection, transportation, and accommodation, in any way contravene his own separationist principle and that of Vatian II. As he would contend (although never expressly), he is welcomed and accorded honors and facilities as a sovereign only in order that he can carry out his role as pastor of huge flocks. Nor was the pope ever visibly uncomfortable when flowers were thrown in his way in Poland, when palm branches were strewn before him between the Basilica of the Immaculate Conception in Washington, D.C., and nearby Trinity College for Women, nor when Handel's *Messiah* (the "Hallelujah Chorus") was sung to greet him (e.g., in Accra in May 1980 and in Manila in February 1981).[85]

Evangelization, Education, and Philanthropy. The pope is insistent on the right to evangelize in all lands, Muslim and Hindu included, although he knows the problem of evangelization is as difficult in those lands as in most Soviet bloc and other communist lands. He interrelates education and evangelization, repeating in many circumstances that childhood catechesis must be continued in lifelong education and culture. In 1980 he awarded the John XXIII International Peace Prize at Kumasi, Ghana, to catechists from the six countries of his first African visitation. Yet John Paul is unequivocal in upholding the right of non-Catholic Christians and non-Christians to spread their version of the Christian faith or their non-Christian faith in lands where Catholicism is still preponderant. He fully endorsed, for example, the formation of the Brazilian Council of

---

84. At an ecumenical meeting in Porto Alegre on 4 July 1980, the leader of a major Pentecostal group in Brazil, while wishing the pope well on his pilgrimage, declined to attend the meeting because of "triumphalist overtones." In a comparable gathering in Paris on 31 May 1980, it was Professor Georges Casalis who raised the church-state issue. As for a triumphalist Catholic Church, John Paul, with his ascetic ideal and deep moral sense, has frequently acknowledged and deplored the excesses of the Church in the past; and in Westminster Cathedral on 28 May 1982, he said on his first day in Britain: "I come at the service of unity in love, in the humble and realistic love of *the repentant fisherman*" (*L'Osservatore Romano*, English ed., 31 May 1982, p. 1; cf. John 21:15).
85. *L'Osservatore Romano*, 19 February 1980, p. 3 (which cites John 15:15 and Mark 10:21); *L'Osservatore Romano*, 10 May 1980, p. 3.

Churches (an entity initiated by his Brazilian bishops) and the Nigerian Christian Association.

John Paul would like not only to see the parochial school system strengthened wherever it exists but also to urge rectors and professors to recover the evangelical mission of the Catholic college, university, and higher institutes of studies. In his directive for seminaries, and especially in his *Sapientia christiana*,[86] for higher education he comes close to obliging all Catholic professors, whether lay or clerical, whether in Catholic or state universities, to heed the teaching of the Church *on man*. In this position he goes even further than Vatican II in holding that the Church has a fairly well-rounded doctrine of man, who was created in the image of God, has fallen but is redeemed, is a sovereign person with free will, rights, responsibilities, and an eternal destiny.[87]

Under the perhaps somewhat reluctant leadership of William Cardinal Baum, prefect of the Sacred Congregation for Catholic Education and formerly archbishop of Washington, there may well be, under the most recent directive, a partial return to older patterns of cloistered diocesan seminary life in curriculum and devotional discipline from the free mingling of seminarians with lay Catholics and other Christians that had come about since Vatican II. The New Code of Canon Law[88] prevents not only government but also university administrators and peer associations from functioning in the maintenance of religious standards of scholarship, which are independent both of the episcopate and the state. First World Catholics criticize this section of the New Code as retrogressive, especially those in North America, who are accustomed to professional-regional accreditation and counsel in promotion.

The pope seems to be quite serious in his call for continuous dialogue with the scholars in the natural sciences and, as a gesture of reconciliation, anticipates as momentously symbolic the predictable vindication of Galileo Galilei on the 350th anniversary of his condemnation by the Roman Inquisition (1633).[89] In the dialogue with other Christians and within the Church, how-

---

86. For the English text of this address, see *Acta Apostolicae Sedis* 71 (30 April 1979):433-35.

87. Williams, *The Mind of John Paul II*, pp. 342-45.

88. See esp. canons 763, 765, and 767 of the code. Canon 767 was modeled on provisions of nineteenth-century concordats with Germany or with its constituent states. Concerning the New Canon Law in general, see Williams, "John Paul II's Concepts of Church, State, and Society," fn. 7.

89. The pope's Alitalia airplane to Argentina bore the astronomer's name.

ever, John Paul is not dialectical or dialogic about the emergence of truth. He is impatient with disputation and personal opinion. For him, therefore, education and evangelization are best held firmly in the hands of the representatives of the magisterium in each country.

John Paul does not hold that tax support of parochial schools (or, commonly elsewhere, religion in state schools) contravenes the principle of church-state separation (or fairness for all confessions). He sent Secretary of State Casaroli to Hartford, Connecticut, on 3 August 1982 for the centenary of the founding of the Knights of Columbus. The pope was prospectively pleased that President Reagan would on this occasion support tax credits for parents of private school pupils and a constitutional amendment permitting officially sanctioned school prayer. Seven cardinals were present, including Archbishop Jaime Sin of Manila. The papal representative lunched with the president, and one wonders whether the former stressed in the conversation the president's school and prolife statements, strongly applauded by almost all Catholics present, or the nuclear freeze, favored by the pope and by the majority of American bishops but opposed in his speech by the president as he took thought of the impending resolution in Congress on one of two nuclear policies.

From almost his earliest writings, Karol Wojtyla has liked to use the term "paraliturgical devotions," by which he has in mind primarily the great processions connected with the Marian year held at the Polish national shrine, Czestochowa, and at Kalwaria Zebrzydowska in his own former diocese, a place he frequented from his boyhood to his nostalgic return to Poland in June 1979 as pope. Corpus Christi Day processions are also involved, as well as such devotions within the Catholic Church as the Adoration of the Reserved Host. John Paul rightly holds that a religion that sets its date of Easter in relation to the vernal equinox and the full moon is a religion of the open sky and the public domain and not merely of the inner space of the contemplative sanctuary. He therefore insists that the Church has the right of manifesting itself publicly. The Solidarity of Workers and Dissenters in Poland succeeded in getting the mass on the radio when the hierarchy failed; the Polish bishops themselves, however, never acquiesced in strictures on paraliturgical manifestations, as did, much earlier, the revived Patriarchal Church in the Soviet Union (1917/18).

As for philanthropy, it was the generosity of ancient Christians, even toward those not their own, that drew mostly favora-

ble attention to them in the pre-Constantinian age, except for
the accusation of Celsus that the Christian concern for orphans
and the poor was more to gain converts than to help the needy.
Catholicism has to this day a vast array of eleemosynary orders,
agencies, and organizations. Since Vatican II, Catholic coopera-
tion with similar non-Catholic bodies, religious or secular, has
been unquestioned and outstanding. In countries of the Second
World, as with Caritas under the Nazis, there is an ideological
opposition to having any religious or other body interfere in
eleemosynary activities, from hospitals to orphanages, one of the
principal outlets for the Christian desire to aid persons in need.
In many states, Christians are often expressly excluded from
even participating at any important decision-making level in the
comparable agencies of the state, although this tendency has
been least true in Poland (except under martial law) and in
Hungary. At the same time, it is lamentable that the Istituto per
le opere di religione (the Vatican bank under Archbishop Paul
C. Marcinkus) should have been permitted under John Paul II
to engage in "high" international speculation, to give (indirectly) allegedly great sums to Solidarity qua organization, and
to promote other quasi-political actions that would appear to go
much beyond the sober financial transactions of a sovereign state
and disinterested humanitarian Caritas.

*The Family, Contraception, Abortion: The Rights of Women as
Mothers.* Marriage, sexual ethics, the chaste celibacy of the religious (male and female), the dignity and even the spirituality of
work, and international intrasocial peace are the outstanding
concerns of John Paul as ethicist. On marriage, John Paul's
thinking is most fully embodied in his apostolic exhortation
Familiaris consortio.[90] Leaving to one side his theology of celibacy, which is closely linked to his eschatology,[91] and his theology of sexuality and marriage, one singles out in the present
context his Charter of Family Rights,[92] which is directed "against
the intolerable usurpations of society and the State,"[93] and his
grounding of these rights in the kingship of the *triplex munus*

---

90. For an English translation of *Familiaris consortio* (promulgated on 22 November
1981), see *L'Osservatore Romano*, English ed., 21-28 December 1981, pp. 1-19. Concerning the notion of the family as a domestic church, see Williams, "John Paul II's Concepts of Church, State, and Society," at fn. 23.
91. See George Huntston Williams, "The Ecumenism of John Paul II," *Journal of
Ecumenical Studies* 19 (Fall 1982), esp. §1.
92. *Familiaris consortio*, §46.
93. Ibid.

Christi,[94] an office which, with the others, devolves in varying modalities upon the people of God and, most fully, of course, on the pope and bishops. Kingship, however, devolves on the royal priestly laity to such an extent that it can be said with respect to them that "the social and political role is included in the kingly mission of service in which Christian couples share by virtue of the sacrament of marriage, and they receive both a command which they cannot ignore and a grace which sustains and stimulates them."[95] In a similar vein, in *Laborem exercens* John Paul converted the curse of pain in childbirth into the insufficient "recognition on the part of society and of their own families" of "the toil of women as mothers"[96] and called for "a social reevaluation of the mother's role of the toil [not pain] connected with it," so that *"true advancement"* would require labor to be restructured in such a way that "women do not have to pay for their advancement by abandoning what is specific to them."[97]

Although it was a severe dominical injunction that the true believer in Jesus (as the Messiah) should let kith and kindred go,[98] one later repeated in a famous hymn of Martin Luther's, the fact is that Christianity, like Judaism, came to think of itself among other things as a religion that defends the family and the authority of the parents, particularly that of the father. However this tendency came about in Christianity in general and then in Protestantism, the development has been fully completed in Vatican II and especially in the thought of John Paul so that, far from being the last of the seven sacraments, as in Peter Lombard (d. 1160), marriage is today coordinate with ordination in marking two main ways for the Christian pilgrim. The domestic church (*ecclesiola, seminarium*) is one of the nine meanings of church;[99] it is, however, also quasi-political as a kind of *municipiolum* in which the parents (especially the father) bear authority. In traditional Catholic and Protestant catechesis the commandment to honor father and mother is the *locus classicus* for both magisterial and paternal authority. Vatican II and especially John Paul, however, take cognizance of the fact that not all peoples of the earth acknowledge the successive revelations in the Old and the New Testament. Nevertheless, from the Cath-

---

94. See Williams, "John Paul II's Concepts of Church, State, and Society," at fn. 55.
95. *Familiaris consortio*, §47.
96. *Laborem exercens*, §9; see also Williams, *The Mind of John Paul II*, p. 287.
97. Ibid., §19.
98. See the related harsh statements, even unto hate of father, in Matthew 10:34-39, Luke 12:51-53, Luke 14:25-27, and Luke 17:33.
99. See Williams, "John Paul II's Concepts of Church, State, and Society," at fn. 20.

olic point of view, especially marked during Vatican II, the
Incarnation of the eternally begotten Son of God as Jesus Christ
is understood to have altered human nature generically so that in
the Second Adam the original image of God in every person,
from conception, has been restored, as in Genesis 1:26. With the
conviction that all human nature since the Incarnation is *simul
lapsa et redempta* ("At once fallen and redeemed"),[100] John Paul,
perhaps even more vehemently than Paul VI and surely with
much more frequency, insists that the unborn bear the image of
the Almighty and are inviolable. Hence he will not hear of abortion as a civil liberty of the pregnant mother, even when
impregnated against her will by rape or incest.[101]

John Paul II on Church and State: A Summary

John Paul II is a revolutionary when his promulgated ascetic
ideal is seen in the context of church history, but not in the context of liberation theology. In the early church, Christians were
regarded as saints, not in the moral sense, but as being God's
ongoing Israel or the New Israel in Jesus Christ. By the Con-
stantinian age, clergy and laity were clearly distinguishable, with
presumptively higher moral standards applying to the clergy. At
the same time the more conscientious and ascetic laymen, heirs
of rigorism, surviving from the age of persecution, withdrew
into the desert in quiet or sometimes vociferous protest against
the accommodation not only of the often nominally Christian
laity, but also of their priests and bishops, to the assignments of
empire. Eventually, these priests and bishops would be called the
secular clergy, not in a disparaging sense but only in the descrip-
tive sense of their laboring as pastors of the flocks engaged in
society and related to its structures. Eventually, especially in the
Latin West, the monastic laymen became themselves also priests,
no longer satisfied with a few among them ordained to the priesthood to make possible their daily masses and splendid liturgies.
They became known, in contrast to the secular clergy of parish
and diocese, as regular priests, because they lived according to
one rule (*regula*) or another. By the end of the eleventh century

---

100. Cf. Martin Luther's *Christian* believer: *simul justus et peccator* ("At once justified
and a sinner").
101. The pope persists in his defense of natural family planning within even the most
squalid of *favelas* of Latin America and amid even the desperate food shortages and star-
vation he encountered in the African states that he visited. In Britain, however, he mod-
erated his formulation as opposition to the "contraceptive mentality," to marriages without the intention of progeny.

there were great international congregations of these regular priests. Under Gregory VII the full ascetic ideal of the regular priests of such an order as the Reformed Benedictines of Cluny was imposed upon the secular clergy. Celibacy and continence were required for all priests, in contrast to the practice in the Eastern Church. Many priests in cathedrals and large collegial churches similarly organized themselves as members of an order, calling themselves canons.

The jurisdictional universality of the Latin Church with its crusading outposts in the East was probably saved from excessive nationalization and ethnicization, to which the Orthodox and other Eastern Churches were prone, by this identification of the Church (*ecclesia*) with the universally celibate priesthood (*sacerdotium*).[102]

At Vatican II the laity were accorded a kind of sacerdotal (also royal and prophetic) dignity and were assigned enlarged roles in the Catholic Church, roles comparable to those earlier proclaimed by Luther in his doctrine of the priesthood of all believers. To be sure, up until Vatican II, the Church had, indeed, the counterpart of this notion: the apostolate of the laity. In reconceiving the Church less as the structured mystical body and more as the pilgrim people of God, however, Vatican II greatly enhanced that apostolate in a powerful ecumenical ferment of clerical-lay dialogue and mutuality. Cardinal Wojtyla encouraged this dialogue in his own cathedral parish in Cracow and in the parishes of his metropolitical province. As pope, however, he is now engaged in a severe reformation of the Vatican II reformation. He is moving back in some ways in order to move ahead with most of the global body of Catholics intact and under discipline in a more literal construction or even conservative reading of the often somewhat ambiguous documents of the council, even with all their sonority and hope.

The ecclesio-political significance of the renewal under John Paul of the ascetic motif among clerics, nuns, married couples, and youth is that we are witnessing an extraordinary process in Catholicism: the "sacerdotalizing" of the laity, that is, the upholding of the ideal of the self-sacrificial celibate priest, who is on the way to sanctification, *mutatis mutandis* for the Christian family, which is thought of as domestic *ecclesiola*. For the pope, as has been noted,[103] the betrothal ideal differs only in the way

---

102. See Williams, "John Paul II's Concepts of Church, State, and Society," at fn. 24.
103. See ibid., at fn. 20.

in which God's love is restrained or responsibly expressed. Sectarian Protestantism can understand this idea. Indeed, the term for the "church of the home" or intimate devout circle, *ecclesiola*, was used by Lutheran Pietists, and it found its counterpart in the Wesleyan class meeting, in both cases originally within the context of the overarching established church, whether of Saxony or of England.

If the great theological issue of the Reformation era was justification by faith alone by the hearing of the Scripture alone, that of the pontificate of John Paul is personal sanctification in whichever of the two ways life unfolds: in service in the sacerdotal ministry or in the lay apostolate. The pope at almost every ecumenical gathering stresses moral as well as doctrinal differences still to be overcome. The moral reference is largely to the sexual ethic once ascribed to the Puritans and Pietists that is now becoming *papally* normative for Catholics (although the pope would not immediately acknowledge the historical parallel without examination of the monographic literature). In the meantime, the most ecumenical of Christian denominations, gathered into the World Council of Churches or national counterparts, have become, because of several kinds of revolution in Western and particularly in Anglo-American societies, decidedly less "puritan" and even somewhat less scriptural than the pope. On the issue of sexual ethics the pope is much closer to evangelicals of various degrees of conservatism and even to fundamentalists and their counterparts elsewhere (particularly as these denominations have penetrated the Third World) than to these ecumenists of the World Council. This distance on the part of the pope from the ecumenists is especially true for those whose presuppositions and motivations go back to the Life and Work tributary (as distinguished from that of Faith and Order) in the development of the means and modalities of ecumenical dialogue with Catholics. It was from the ranks of these ecumenists that most of the acceptances came to send observers to Vatican II.

The Roman Catholic Church, amid its global commitments, and with its vast network of orders and diocesan provinces held together by an apostolic mission to many states and to all national hierarchies, is, under the strenuous leadership of John Paul, in the process of assuming some of the sociological and *psychological* characteristics of a "sect," namely, moral rigorism and tightened discipline with respect to seminarians, priests, female religious, the family and various religiously established institutions, such as schools and universities, scholarly publications and the mass media, hospitals and philanthropies, youth groups, migrants, the underprivileged, and the imperiled. Such a world organization represents, especially at the level of clerical leadership, the benign superimposition on the societies of the world of the standards of a sacramentally bound spiritual, universal community, a social organism pulsating throughout the globe with renewed vitality from its center in Vatican City, a body overlaying and interpenetrating many parts of all Three Worlds and influencing the councils of the nations.

In John Paul there are, accordingly, several variations on the church-state theme. To the extent that he retains or recovers the full loyalty of celibate priests and monial and conventual auxiliaries, fosters adequate fresh vocations for the next generation, and persuades lay Catholics of all conditions directly when on pilgrimage, through the *sacerdotium*, and by a cascade of communications, the Roman Catholic Church will come more and more to appear like an immense and cohesive sect or a grand order, one conforming less and less to the world (Romans 12:2) while being committed to serving and saving it.

Catholicism under the Polish pope will be less indulgent toward indigenization and diversity of theological opinion than it was during the Middle Ages in Europe and toward indigenization in catechesis and rituals during the phenomenal missionary expansion of Catholicism in the Age of the Counterreformation. Except in its positions concerning the natural sciences, theological scholarship, and nuclear and conventional war, Catholicism under John Paul tends to show affinities with the Moral Majority, with which only a fraction of American Catholics feel wholly sympathetic.

Despite some anger or restlessness and disappointment in several sectors of the Catholic Church, the Polish pontiff is clearly disciplining and perfecting a system that obliges Catholics, other Christians, and non-Christians, indeed political theorists, statesmen, and politicians, to think through the church-state problematic in fresh ways. Already the differentiation is great during his pontificate between the universal episcopal *sacerdotium*, at its center a sovereign state, and the lower priesthood, the monial and conventual sisterhoods, and the quasi-ecclesial families of sovereign persons in global reaction and response to the new call for a Catholic pietism, a Catholic puritanism under the persuasive guidance of the charismatic successor of Peter and the discerning, sovereign Vicar of Christ.

The title *Vicarius Christi*, of Byzantine imperial origin, was

assumed by some popes from the eighth century and became a
fixed papal title in the eleventh. One can summarize, therefore,
with a slight adaptation of the 494 dictum of Pope Gelasius I,
now that his *mundus* of the shrinking Mediterranean empire has
become indeed the *globus orbis terrestris* circumnavigable in the
air by his successor: "Duo quippe sunt . . . quibus mundus hic
regitur: auctoritas sacrata pontificum et saeculares potestates"
("There are two [orders] . . . by which this world is principally
ruled: the sacred authority *of the popes* and the secular [i.e., im-
perial] powers").[104] Gelasius believed in the separation of church
and state and would therefore, after blinking at the immensity of
his successor's world, probably agree with John Paul II that, for
the sacred authority of bishops to be exercised around the globe,
the *Sovrano*, the *Pontifex Maximus*, must also exercise that precise degree of sovereignty to make possible his universal apostolic presence by appointing bishops, sending nuncios, or being
himself collegially present and presiding among local conferences of bishops or among them convened representatively at
Rome.

The present-day church historian may add also that, unlike
most sectarian rigorism, which from being merely strenuous in
the faith can often become stern, judgmental, and even persecu-
tory or bellicose, the new ascetic ideal of the Catholic Church
under John Paul represents an extraordinary mutation in that it
has a theology of and respect for the body, full sexuality within
the family, and the dignity of work. At the same time, this
"ascetic" Church in a re-formation of a council-wrought reform,
in its relationship to society and the state, far from being pessimistic, wishes to serve the world in a concern grounded in the
Incarnation and hence in the hope for global peace and social
harmony before the Second Advent. It is a Church that under
John Paul, the conservative implementer of Vatican II, places
emphasis on persuasion, tolerance, respect for the dignity of
every person, love for the global neighbor, compassion for both
fellow human beings and for nature. On this less jurisdictional
and more dialogic level this reformed Church is also unhurriedly
but authentically ecumenical as well as universal.

This Church will not seek to reinstitute the pre-Vatican thesis
that the state, when the Roman Catholic Church is in the
majority, must serve the Church. Rather, in the spirit of John

---

104. For Gelasius's actual saying, see Andreas Thiel, ed., *Epistolae Romanorum Pontificium*, 2 vols. (Braunschweig: E. Peter, 1868), 1:350ff.; see also Williams, "John Paul II's
Concepts of Church, State and Society," p. 470.

XXIII, and true to the main directives of Vatican II, the Church under John Paul II will continue to serve the world and all its peoples. For all his spirituality, and perhaps through the clarity gained therefrom, however, John Paul II is also very much a political as well as a pastoral pope with an eschatological sense at once fearless, hopeful, and grave.[105]

---

105. For several of the issues discussed in this essay, and much more, see the only interview with John Paul granted thus far, given to André Frossard, biographer of Charles de Gaulle, and published as the book *N'ayez pas peur!* [*Be Not Afraid !*] (Paris: Robert Laffont, 1982).

Bibliographical Essay

Almost all books on the pope contain something on his view of church, state, and society. Leaving to one side the many sumptuous albums of pictures with texts that came out at the time of the election of Karol Wojtyla, many of them still rich in documentation of his prepapal life, one turns in chronological order to the biographies, some also illustrated, that appeared later. The books mentioned below are fairly well limited to English titles. Variant titles are supplied if these came out simultaneously in different countries from different publishers.

Possibly the first work was that of the Reverend Dr. Joseph P. Locigno, of partly Polish ancestry as well as Italian, *We Have a Pope* (New York: Manor Books, 1978). The acerb and perceptive, sometime Jesuit, Peter Hebblethwaite placed the election of Karol Wojtyla in perspective in his *The Year of Three Popes* (London and Cleveland: Collins, 1979), which clarifies factors in the choice of a Pole. The American Msgr. Ludvik Nemec, of Czech ancestry, wrote as a Slavophile enthusiast and covered Wojtyla's life to the installation in *Pope John Paul II: A Festive Profile* (New York: Catholic Publishing House, 1979), with illustrations. Its rough counterpart in popular appeal, also without notes, is that of the Sydney-born journalist James Oram, *The People's Pope: The Story of Karol Wojtyla of Poland* (San Francisco: Chronicle Books, 1979), which carries the account through *Redemptor hominis*. One may group together Michael O'Carroll, S.S.Sp., *Poland and John Paul II* (Dublin: Veritas, 1979), and Mary Craig, *Man from a Far Country: A Portrait of Pope John Paul II* (London and Sydney: Hodder and Stoughton, 1979); both authors were fascinated by the Polish background, on which they sought with resourcefulness to inform themselves, although without direct use of the pope's native language.

Another brace of books came precisely from Poles, the Reverend Dr. Mieczyslaw Maliński and the publicist exile, George Blazynski. Maliński, currently a priest of St. Florian's in Cracow, had been a seminary friend of the pope, with whom Maliński later spent time in Rome during Vatican Council II and then as a temporary academic colleague at the Catholic University of Lublin (in Great Britain, Mieczyslaw Maliński, *Pope John Paul II: The Life of My Friend Karol Wojtyla*, trans. P. S. Falla [London: Burns and Oakes, 1979]; in the United States, *Pope John Paul II: The Life of Karol Wojtyla* [New York: Seabury Press, 1979; Garden City, N.Y.: Image, 1982]). Maliński's book tended to interpret the pope as more theologically progressive than perhaps His Holiness desired. In any case, some of the purported verbatim conversations of Wojtyla at the Polish College after the council sessions bordered on indiscretion from one who in his British title wished to be known as a "friend." In addition, however, it distressed many who knew of Maliński's truly close relationship with the pope that the press secretary of the Vatican declared *en passant* that "the author's only connection with the pope is that he is a priest in Cracow." Maliński moved informingly back and forth from the current to the past in a vivid but not always clear presentation, the existential account based primarily on memories and the author all the more poignantly excited because he was on a study tour in West Germany at the time that the news broke of the election. (The Polish version, Mieczyslaw Maliński, *Droga do Watykanu Jana Pawla II* [Rzym: Nakl. Ksiezy Marianow, 1979], which was composed afterwards, is chronological and smaller.) Blazynski, in *John Paul II: A Man from Cracow* (London: Weidenfeld, 1979), took time to do some substantial research and presented a coherent picture, especially for those not familiar with Poland.

There is another brace of accounts, one "by his American friend," John M. Szotak, *In the Footsteps of Pope John Paul II: An Intimate Portrait* (Englewood Cliffs, N.J.: Prentice-Hall, 1980), and the other by five benign critics, Hebblethwaite among them (in Great Britain, John Whale, ed., *The Pope from Poland: An Assessment* [London: Collin, 1980]; in the United States, John Whale and Peter Hebblethwaite, eds., *The Man Who Leads the Church: An Assessment of John Paul II* [San Francisco: Harper and Row, 1980]). Although most of the authors are Catholic, they among the first sounded the alarm about conservative traits and policies evident behind the charismatic teacher of firm doctrine and behavior.

Another brace of books appeared in America, the first by this author (*The Mind of John Paul II: Origins of His Thought and Action* [New York: Seabury Press, 1981]), the other by historian and sometime editor of *The New Statesman*, Paul Johnson (*Pope John Paul II and the Catholic Restoration* [New York: St. Martin's Press, 1981]), who was then on leave in Washington, D.C., at the American Enterprise Institute for Public Policy Research. Johnson dedicated the volume to the members of the institute. Johnson's dust jacket, which uses a fuller version of the same Karsh portrait that appears on the jacket of *The Mind of John Paul II*, mentions the attempt upon the pope's life on 13 May

1981, by which time the substantial work had been readied for the press. One of the most scholarly books to appear in any language, Johnson's volume is limited largely to what the pope has said in languages accessible to a scholarly writer without Polish. Only sketchily rehearsing the Polish background, Johnson approvingly describes and analyzes the ways in which the pope has swiftly restored the Catholic Church in discipline and outlook so far as he can, in keeping with what would be a very conservative reading of the achievements of Vatican II in terms of polity and politics. The book is replete with insights and facts on church, state, and society. The author uses several of the English writers mentioned above but does not seem to have drawn upon the resources and diverse points of view accessible to him during his American sojourn. He does not cite this author's work, which is known to have been at the institute during Johnson's visit (which was apparently cut short by illness).

Johnson's work is more systematic than chronological in structure. Referring to Father Antonio Rosmini-Serbati's *Delle cinque piaghe della Santo Chiesa* (1848; for an English translation, see *Of the Five Wounds of the Holy Church*, ed. H. P. Liddon [London: Rivingstons, 1883]), Johnson, at the core of his tripartite book, identifies the "five evils of the age" that the pope presently addresses: "the crucifixion of man, the temptation of violence, secularization by stealth, imperilled certitudes, and the shadow of heresy." Alert to the fact that the pope "positively hates determinism," Johnson sees him with perceptive approval eschewing two false roads, one leading to the drawbridge and the fortress church, the other to "a church of compromise, with enough relaxation of rigour to keep the indifferent . . . , and enough intellectual spice to attract the educated." The proper road of the pope is toward Christian humanism without suspicion of *religiosidad popular*, so long as the latter does not become syncretistic; John Paul himself is an exponent of the religion of the mind as well as of the heart, religion responsive to the stirrings of local tradition. In sum, according to Johnson: "With all the strength of his faith, and all the power of his intellect, and all the magic of his personality, he is striving to rebuild the authority of the Papacy."

Unlike St. Martin's Press, which put out Johnson's *Catholic Restoration*, Seabury Press, which put out *The Mind of John Paul II*, may well have been the first commercial (non-Polish) publishing house in the New World to have attempted to do justice to the plethora of Polish diacritical marks. What follows below is a correction of selected errors that appear in *The Mind of John Paul II;* the author has limited himself to those that have bearing on the themes in the present monograph:

Page 61, lines 24-26: For "Cavalier) . . . Niżyński, would" read "Cavalier). This work had been commissioned by the founder of Studio 39, Juliusz Kudliński (b. 1898), who sought a workshop for the mingling of professionals and amateurs. The composer, Marian Niżyński, would"

Page 65, lines 15-16: For "called . . . group, with" read "kept in touch with some five other conspiratorial groups. These groups, with"

Page 65, line 26: For "under Kotlarczyk" read "under Kwiatowski"

Page 65, line 32: For "1945 to 1953" read "1953 to 1957"

Page 65, lines 36-37: For "recited . . . Occupation the" read "recited *or heard recited* in the Rhapsodic Theatre or in other groups: patriots boycotted Nazi Polish theatre. During the Occupation alone the"

Page 65, line 38: For "productions" read "presentations"

Page 66, lines 7-8: For "by Zegadlowicz . . . Wadowice" read "by Jan Kasprowicz (d. 1926), socialist turned Christian, *Hymny*"

Page 68, line 24: For "(see chapter 21, part 3" read "(see chapter 2, part 3)"

Page 88, line 25: For "took place . . . 1944" read "took place from 1 August through 2 September 1944"

Page 88, line 27: For "7 September" read "7 August"

Page 235, line 42: For "from therter" add "from the vantage point of the seething center of the world's largest archdiocese, a supporter"

Page 415: After "Wyspiański" add "Wyszyński, Stefan 143, 165, 175, 234, 255; on church-state relations xiv, 28, 30-31, 221, 230-31, 251, 255, 324"

In response to one portion of a long review of the author's book by Boleslaw Taborski in *Tygodnik Powszechny,* 1 August 1982, three members of the papal commission on papal publications headed by the Reverend Dean Marian Jaworski, all of whom the author knows personally and in whose offices he has been, declared in a letter to the editor in *Tygodnik Powszechny,* 26 September 1982, that the author's alleged data concerning the genesis and alterations from Polish into English of *Osoba i Czyn (The Acting Person)* were not so much interesting (as Taborski had written) as *dezinformacja.* This word, from so high a source, suggests *intentional* misrepresentation. This author, however, was depending wholly on Wojtyla's preface in the publication itself and on archival information printed in the *Bulletin* of the institute under whose auspices the English version had appeared in Holland and the United States in February 1979 (see above, p. 6, fn. 18). During the preparation of his book, the author had no "inside" information from, and almost no contact with, Cardinal Wojtyla's American phenomenological collaboratrice of Polish noble ancestry and depended for his assertion that the English version was "definitive" on what Wojtyla himself said on two pages of front matter. It is therefore personally reassuring that the Vatican version, *Persona e Atto* (Vatican City: Libreria Vaticana, 1982), which retains two of the original three English prefaces and includes a new one by Armando Rigobello, states that the version is "according to the definitive: *The Acting Person*" and makes no mention, as does the German version, as being from "a second Polish edition." This author is thus presumably absolved of having given *dezinformacja.* It is, in any case, of more interest to English-reading persons to understand what the author clarified about the three versions in English of *The Acting Person,* chapter seven. This chapter (in whatever version) is most important for papal views of society and about the two versions of a closely related article; see above, p. 6, fn. 18.

The final brace of books is striking indeed by their contrast, status, and intended readerships, one for Americans, the other for Britons, both papally authorized. The first is a comic-book story of the papal superman, known to have been sanctioned by His Holiness and with the text copyrighted by Father Maliński, *The Life of Pope John Paul II: The Entire Story! From His Childhood to the Assassination Attempt!* (New York: Marvel Comics Group, 1982); it is called "volume one, number one" in what may be a projected series at intervals. In a country of a large Jewish population the only reference to the Holocaust is in one panel on page fourteen, where a Nazi overseer of the Solvay Works is seen and heard saying: "Wojtyla! You may enter!" In the foreground, two other workers, one smoking, converse before reaching the quarry: "There was another raid last night— just down the street. Jews, I think, in hiding." His fellow worker responds: "Poor devils! I've heard of a place near Auschwitz they are sent to." This town of terror, which in Polish is Oświecim, can be seen from the towers of Cracow cathedral. Such is all there is about the monstrous genocide in a booklet of sixty-four pages, with about seven panels to a page.

In marked contrast in format and intention is the stately souvenir volume, harking back to the first splendid albums, prepared by Lord Longford for the "pastoral and ecumenical pilgrimage to the United Kingdom." Many of the pictures from prepapal days are here for the first time; some family pictures and views of the pope in the Vatican and Castel Gondolfo could only have been made available by the pope himself. The scenes from the pilgrimages are striking. The text is arranged in nine chapters, and again a British author defers primarily to the English writers mentioned above. No Polish persons, except the pope himself, are mentioned in the acknowledgments. Francis

Aungier Pakenham (b. 1905), Seventh Earl of Longford and minister of state in several major capacities, is a biographer of many great figures, from Jesus Christ and Saint Francis of Assisi to Lincoln, Eamon De Valera, Kennedy, and Nixon. The countess of Longford, also a biographer, as sometime trustee of the National Portrait Gallery conceivably counseled her husband on the selection and arrangement of the beautiful colored plates. The book is entitled *Pope John Paul II: An Authorized Biography* (London: Joseph, Rainbird, 1982). As one who served in the Labour government of Ernest Bevin, Lord Longford, writing in the first person, treats perceptively and slightly critically the pope's position on consumerism in Ireland and Britain, which many, now long unemployed, do not feel is on target. Lord Longford suggests that the pope means disdain of "throw-away-ability." In dealing with *Laborem exercens*, Lord Longford does not note its explicit critique of workers' organizing primarily in one party, as, for example, in the Labour party. He does recognize that the pope is not "some kind of diplomatic ally of the Atlantic alliance" (see pp. 190-203). In an "authorized" account of days under the Nazis, Lord Longford says that, "very sympathetic to the predicament of the Jews, Wojtyla . . . contributed to resistance work by supplying them with Aryan identification papers." This fact means that Wojtyla would have supplied Jews with baptismal certificates of departed Catholics, a policy that his archbishop opposed as duplicitous. The claim was first made by the head of B'nai B'rith in Rome in 1978 and is always cited. This author, wishing to find evidence of such compassionate conduct of such personal risk, has searched in vain. It is quite likely that the "authorized biography," actually printed in Verona, profited, however, from the assistance of many more persons and works in Rome and elsewhere than those mentioned or cited by Lord Longford. He concludes with a chapter on "Catholicism in Britain."

At the same time that the pope was authorizing Father Maliński to oversee the text of the American comic book, for the presumptively more sophisticated French the pope granted a series of interviews to Andre Frossard (*N'ayez pas peur!* [Be Not Afraid!] [Paris: Robert Laffont, 1982]). Frossard, a political conservative like Johnson, is the biographer of Charles de Gaulle. The work was immediately translated into Italian. One of its points will be mentioned below in due course. There is also one new papal publication that is almost a papal unicum—the book *À l'image de Dieu, homme et femme, Une Lecture de Genese 1-3*

(Paris: du Cerf, 1980). These fascinating meditations on sexuality, entering into the depths and heights of the subject and quite boldly using modern biblical criticism concerning strands J and E in Genesis, were begun by the cardinal as ethicist before his elevation and were continued in multilingual Wednesday audiences. The status of a book in the scale of papal authority among utterances has not been determined.

Proceeding to the new literature that has appeared since the two articles constituting the present monograph were written, one thinks first of James V. Schall, S.J., *The Church, the State, and Society* (Chicago: Franciscan Herald Press, 1982). This and two other matching paperbacks came out of "The John Paul Synthesis: A Trinity College [Washington, D.C.] Symposium," promoted by William Cardinal Baum. The work is based on the prepapal and papal documentation as of the symposium in 1980 and stresses "no other truth [than the Catholic]," especially in society at large in conservative reaction to what Schall pillories as a mere "sociology of faith" too rampant in the Church. To turn to specific relationships, one thinks of George Bull, *Inside the Vatican* (New York: St. Martin's Press, 1982), a substantial, conservative work with little on the distinctive thrust of John Paul II. This book has the same range as the earlier but more amply historical work by Msgr. Paul Poupard, *Un Pape pour quoi faire? De saint Pierre à Jean-Paul II* (Paris: Mazarine, 1980), which concentrates on events of the twentieth century and changes in the curia; it contains just a bit about John Paul. In two related articles on the Vatican, Francis Xavier Murphy writes on "City of God" and Dennis J. Dunn on " Global Outreach," in *The Wilson Quarterly*, 6 (Autumn 1982):98-123, with two pages of related bibliography. Neither of these writers knew about the seriousness of the financial problems of Vatican City State and the indiscretions of Archbishop Paul Marcinkus with Michael Sindona, now in prison, and with Roberto Calvi of the Banco Ambrosiano, found hanged from a London bridge. Jessica Savitch, in her program for CPB/PBS, "Frontline," makes available the transcript of "God's Banker"(twenty-five pages), a program originally broadcast on 14 February 1983. Malachi Martin, former Jesuit and professor in the Pontifical Biblical Institute, registers a most pessimistic view even about the valiant efforts of John Paul II on the church-state legacy in *The Decline and Fall of the Roman Church* (New York: G. P. Putnam's Sons, 1981).

All these works have something substantial to say about the

Ostpolitik of recent popes, including the present pontiff. The most interesting article from the Soviet position (see above, p. 37, fn. 3) is an article by V. Makhin, "Religion in the Ideological Arsenal of Anticommunism," *Politicheskoe Samoobrazonvanie*, no. 12 (December 1982), pp. 115-22 (this monthly issue is the one carrying the black-framed picture of Leonid Brezhnev and a picture of Yuri Andropov, the issue delayed until 28 December [and summarized by Tass] because of the funeral on 15 November and the subsequent succession). With the world's attention drawn since September to a possible "Bulgarian Connection" in the attempt on the pope's life, with the implied complicity of Andropov, former head of the KGB, one might have expected that Makhin's article could have been temporarily withdrawn. Despite the fact that the pope's two personal representatives shook hands with the former KGB chief at Brezhnev's funeral, Makhin makes of John Paul II "the most political pope" of modern times, with savage intent quoting from him at some length, with special reference to Solidarity. Of only direct value for understanding papal-Soviet relations is *Rapport secret au Comité central sur l'état de l'Eglise en U.R.S.S.*, introduced by Nikita Struve, translated by Serge Benoît (Paris: du Seuil, 1980), which reports to the Central Committee the state of the Orthodox Church in the Soviet Union, revealing more inner strength than commonly accorded the Church.

For papal policy with respect to Lithuania, the English translations of a persecuted Lithuanian secret publication is especially valuable, *The Chronicle of the Catholic Church in Lithuania*, printed by the Lithuanian Roman Catholic Priests' League of America in Brooklyn, N.Y., on roughly a quarterly basis, issues numbered consecutively since its first appearance. Each issue rehearses the same basic history since 1940 and provides a map of Soviet Lithuania, with all the places on it referred to in the detailed accounts of persecution. Number forty-seven contains a letter, dated 20 August 1980, from John Paul to Bishop Steponovocius, who is held in internal exile from his proper see of Vilnius and who might by the cardinal whom the pope is said to have named *in petto*. Bishop Luidvikas Povilonis was permitted to go to Rome to work out an arrangement whereby the Soviet authorities would reinstate two bishops, including that of Vilnius, in return for acquiescence in the installation of bishops acceptable to the Soviet authorities. The clandestine magazine pleads with the pope not to make any compromise and thereby leave unvindicated those who have suffered so much, clerical and lay, women and men, for the true faith. Before the near disgrace of Lithuanian Marcinkus, there was great hope that the archbishop might come to Soviet Lithuania for one of its two centenaries, either the one in 1984 (the fifth centenary of the death of patron Saint Casimir) or the one in 1987-88 (the sixth centenary of the conversion of the Lithuanians to Latin Christianity). The current issue, number fifty-six, presents the text of a petition of over four hundred priests, dated July-August 1982, imploring for religious freedom as guaranteed by the Soviet constitution. There is also an article expressing chagrin that the pope in January 1983 made a Latvian rather than a Lithuanian prelate the first Soviet cardinal.

The most solid study of the Vatican and the Soviet bloc is that of Hansjakob Stehle, *Eastern Politics of the Vatican, 1917-1979* (Athens: Ohio University Press, 1981), which ends with the pontificate of John Paul II. J. Kramer, "The Vatican's Ostpolitik," *Review of Politics* 52 (July 1980):283-308, scarcely carries Stehle's argument further. J. Luxmore, "A Test for the Vatican Ostpolitik," *Month* 15 (December 1982):412-17, however, is specific and up-to-date. As to Poland in particular, there is Richard Spielman, "Avoiding a Showdown in Poland," *Foreign Affairs* 49 (Winter 1982-83):20-36; Spielman seems to reflect the conciliatory tone and realism of the pope's announced intention of visiting Warsaw, Lublin, and Czestochowa, without determined conditions, for the sixth centenary in June 1983 of the translation of the Black Madonna, a visit designed to strengthen the Church under Mary and society and thereby to inhibit a further breakdown of the sense of national solidarity. John Paul knows that he is useful to Wojciech Jaruzelski, just as he can help to prevent despair among the Polish people and the Church.

The visits of the pope to Central America—Costa Rica on 2-3 March 1983, Nicaragua on 4 March, Panama on 5 March, El Salvador on 6 March, Guatemala on 7 March, Honduras on 8 March, and Haiti on 9 March—involved him in several kinds of church-state relations. In American-influenced Panama he stressed again his sexual ethics, from contraception to divorce. In Nicaragua he found that the five priests in the government had refused to comply with his request to leave office (see G. Palumbo, "Papal Letter Enters Nicaragua Church-State Fray," *National Catholic Reporter*, 27 August 1982, p. 19). One priestly incumbent was out of the country; the pope's most conspicuous encounter was with Culture Minister Ernesto Cardenal, who, kneeling before the pope, was prevented from kissing his ring.

Cardenal received instead a fingering rebuke—an act altogether uncharacteristic of the pontiff, with his high sense of the personal dignity of every man, presumably therefore of a refractory priest. The pope's mass was interrupted by shouts of anguish that he did not include in his prayers the Sandinista soldiers recently slain, these shouts amid heckling evidently permitted or promoted by the government. John Paul may have weakened the Church further by dividing it when he disparagingly named the supporters of the Sandinistas the "national or popular church." In El Salvador the pope distanced himself somewhat from American policy when he called for a "dialogue for peace" from which "no one should be excluded." By visiting the tomb of Archbishop Oscar Romero secretly and then by announcing that he had done so, John Paul made up for his strangely *pro forma* tribute to the martyr in Rome in 1980. In Guatemala he faced as head of state a charismatic, twice-born, totalitarian Protestant who had refused clemency for six political prisoners before his arrival. In this country he had to deal with totalitarianism, violence, and a large Indian population subject to continual harassment. In Belize, encountering again a large proportion of Spanish Protestants, the pope called for unity. In Haiti he ended the *patronato* and supported the bishops in their first attempts to criticize the government for its repressive ways.

Penny Lernoux, *Cry of the People: United States Involvement in the Rise of Fascism, Torture, and Murder, and the Persecution of the Catholic Church in Latin America* (Garden City, N.Y.: Doubleday, 1980) provides the large context for Catholic church-state relations in Latin America, as does, from the conservative side, James V. Schall, S.J., ed., *Liberation Theology in Latin America* (San Francisco: Ignatius Press, 1982), a collection of essays and documents, the latter papal and otherwise. Tommie Sue Montgomery, *Revolution in El Salvador* (Boulder, Colo.: Westview Press, 1982), deals with one of the three main problem countries visited by the pope. Maryknoll Father Stephen De Mott describes the visit of the pope to one in "Report from Two Nicaraguas," *Christianity and Crisis* 43 (18 April 1983):133-34. De Mott and his Maryknoll colleague Paul Newpower cover the papal visits to Nicaragua and Honduras, El Salvador and Guatemala, in "The Pope's Trip," *St. Anthony's Messenger*, June 1983, forthcoming, while De Mott tells the story fully of "The Church in Nicaragua," *Maryknoll Magazine*, 77 (August 1983), forthcoming.

For papal relations with Israel, sources are in chronic short supply. However, on the eve of an incompleted trip of Yitsak Shamir to the Holy See, possibly looking for a new basis for relations, *Ma-Ariv* for 6 March 1981 carried seven columns on "Relations between the Catholic Church and Israel." At the National Workshop on Jewish-Christian Relations, held in Boston on 26 April 1983, Msgr. William Murphy, undersecretary of the Pontifical Commission on Justice and Peace, read a paper on "The Middle East Conflict," which said that the Holy See would have no problem "in principle" in establishing diplomatic relations with Israel. The paper made clearer the position taken since 1967 with respect to Jerusalem, no longer insisting on "internationalization" but simply on "international guarantees" regardless of what state has "political dominion." Msgr. Secretary Jorge Mejía, of the Vatican Commission for Religious Relations with Judaism, gave at Seton Hall University on 2 May 1983 another related paper, "Pope John Paul II and the Jews." These two papers will probably appear in *Origins*. A complementary paper, which will also no doubt be published, is that of Professor Joseph L. Ryan, S.J., "Palestinian Rights: Resonances in the Life and Themes of Pope John Paul II," delivered at the Fifth U.N. Seminar on the Inalienable Rights of the Palestinian People held in New York in March 1982. George Irani is preparing a doctoral dissertation at the University of Southern California, "The Papacy and the Middle East: The Role of the Vatican in Arab-Israeli Conflict, 1960-1980." This Lebanese-born scholar of extensive training in Milan gathered materials notably in Rome, Beirut, and Jerusalem. In *N'ayez pas peur* John Paul avoided answering questions about the State of Israel. In the French Jewish monthly, *L'Arche*, 12 December 1982, pp. 72-75, Frossard was interviewed about this lack in a piece entitled, somewhat bitterly, since Frossard showed no regrets with the title, "Un pape bien temporel."

Given the pope's injunction against direct priestly resistance of a political character to even terroristic authoritarian regimes, and his counsel to Catholic youth to work for reconciliation and dialogue rather than violent confrontation, it is instructive to see John Paul as himself an idealistic, youthful nationalist of great gifts, between the age of nineteen and twenty-five, a student, mystic, and seminarian, along with at least one priest, Father Siedlecki, whose family apartment and niece, like Karol Wojtyla, are often referred to in any of six conspiratorial theatres in Cracow, with one of which Wojtyla was especially active even after becoming a seminarian. The following works may prove useful:

Mieczyslaw Kotlarczyk, "Teatre Rapsodyczny w latach, 1941-1945," *Pamietnik Teatralny* 12 (1963):155-64.

Juliusz Kudliński, *Dawne i Nowe Przypadki* (Cracow: Wydawnictwo Literackie, 1975), chap. 2.

————, *Mlodosci mej stolica* (Warsaw: Pax, 1970), pp. 386-98.

Tadeusz Kwiatowski, "Krakowski Teatre Konspiracyjny," *Pamietnik Teatralny* 12 (1963):146-54.

Juliusz Kydryński, "Krakowski Teatre Konspiracyjny," *Twórczość* 2 (1946): 171-75.

————, *Uwaga, Gong!* (Cracow: Wydawnictwo Literackie, 1962).

Maria K. Maciejewska, "Bibliografia: Polskie Zycie teatralne podczas Drugiej Wojny Swiatowej," *Pamietnik Teatralny* 12 (1963):71-98.

Stanslaw Sierotwiński, *Krakowskie podziemie literackie pod Okupacja Hitlerowska* (Cracow: Państwowe Wydawn. Naukowe, 1971).

The foregoing citations may serve as a fuller replacement of what the author has given in *The Mind of John Paul II*, p. 359, fnn. 17, 18. The author completed this further research by coincidence on the very day, 18 April 1983, when His Holiness personally took cognizance of the decennial assembly in Rome of the Trilateral Commission. This bibliographical essay ends with a quotation from the sometime Marxist philosopher, Leszek Kolalowski, whom this author met in Warsaw in August 1961, now a convert to Christianity and professor of philosophy at the University of Chicago. Cardinal Wojtyla movingly quoted from him in *Sign of Contradiction* (New York: Seabury Press, 1979), p. 106: "[H]e lists [in 'Jesus Christ, Prophet and Reformer,' 1965] [four] values ['for which world culture is indebted to Christianity']: the supplanting of law in favour of love; the ideal of an end to arrogance in human relationships; the truth that man does not live by bread alone; the abolition of the idea of a chosen people."

Cambridge, Mass., 3 May 1983
Polish Constitution Day (1793)

ADDENDUM

The pope now prepares to leave for Warsaw, Czestochowa, Poznań, Katowice, Wroclaw, Opole, and Cracow on 16-24 June, on an itinerary conspicuously linked to national piety more than to Solidarity, with no advance assurance of an encounter with Walesa, whose own courage and hope was expressed in his address at the Harvard Commencement on 27 May 1983. Gordon Thomas and Max Morgan-Witts set forth an astounding account in *Pontiff* (Garden City: Doubleday, 1983) based on a hundred interviews, mostly in Rome, and on many secret files. They intertwine throughout the lives of Agca of the Gray Wolves, Paul VI, John Paul I, and John Paul II through the assassination attempt of 13 May 1981. This account is the fullest in print concerning Agca and his antipapal hatred among his many hates. The authors accept as proven a letter of the pope to Breshnev, delivered by Marcinkus, threatening to "relinquish the Throne of St. Peter and return to stand at the barricades beside his fellow Poles" (p. 406). Papal renunciation and street violence are wholly out of keeping in one, who even as a youth, eschewed violent resistance under the Nazis and against the Communists. Finding that John Paul II was regularly briefed with CIA information on the USSR and that he was in frequent contact by the telephone with Walesa to keep up his morale and to urge moderation, the authors assert that Andropov "approved the order for Agca to murder the pope." The extraordinary sleuthing brings out confidential information on many church-state and other issues and also certain severe and unpleasant aspects of the papal personality; it also confirms the strongly eschatological strain in John Paul II. Thomas and Morgan-Witts, however, have only made more plausible the motivation of Agca, not of Andropov.

Cambridge, Mass., 14 June 1983

LIBRARY OF DAVIDSON COLLEGE

s on regular loan may be checked   ks